Backgammon

Mannesse Manuscript (14th century): A couple playing backgammon (*Courtesy of The Bettmann Archive*)

Backgammon

The Action Game

*by Prince Alexis Obolensky
and Ted James*

COLLIER BOOKS
A Division of Macmillan Publishing Co., Inc.
NEW YORK

Library of Congress Catalog Card Number: 71-80797

First Collier Books Edition 1969

Fourteenth Printing 1979

Backgammon is also published in a hardcover edition by Macmillan
Publishing Co., Inc.

Macmillan Publishing Co., Inc.
866 Third Avenue, New York, N.Y. 10022

Collier Macmillan Canada, Ltd.

Printed in the United States of America

contents

Introduction

Regardless of what anyone might tell you, backgammon is not played with a racket and you do not buy a backgammon net to keep your cat from falling out of your window. Backgammon is a game, played with dice, a board, and two sets of fifteen men. Most people have heard of it, but until recently few have known how to play. Many associate it with cribbage or parcheesi, and few realize that the other side of a checkerboard is not like the back side of the jack of spades. The other side of many checkerboards is a backgammon board.

Backgammon's history dates back to ancient Sumer, making it probably the oldest game in existence. It was played in one form or another in ancient Egypt, Greece, Rome, Persia, India, China, Japan, Mexico, North America. More recently, it has been played throughout the Eastern and Western worlds.

In addition to its vast history and romance, backgammon can boast of excitement, intrigue, evasiveness, unpredictability, gratification, exasperation, and lightning speed. If you're looking for a game which will get under your skin and stay there, then backgammon is your game.

To begin with, it is a game of skill. The beginner will find that he must devote some time to learning the basic principles and strategies. And as he progresses, he will take this basic knowledge and expand it to fit his own particular kind of game. This learning process will continue for as long as he plays. For example, recently at the world-famous International Backgammon Tournament, held annually at the Lucaya Beach Hotel on Grand Bahama Island, and attended by the most prominent and skillful backgammon players on earth, an entire roomful of champion players watched a replay of one game in which a new kind of strategy was employed. Proof that no matter how long you have played, or how skillful you have become, the game always packs an extra surprise punch.

Introduction

Basically, backgammon is a contest in mathematics. In any given game, the mathematical probabilities, chances, and changes ultimately control the game. The player who possesses superior awareness of these factors will eventually win.

However, to add to the fascination, and at times nurturing exasperation and frustration, backgammon is also a game of chance. Since a roll of the dice determines every move, skill can only be applied after the chance roll of the dice. For this reason, beginners find it especially intriguing. It honestly can be said that a beginner with unusually lucky dice can and will defeat an old pro. This, of course, does not hold true in a series of games, as skill will ultimately win out.

Several years ago, and strictly as a joke, one of the world's greatest players sat down for a match with an eight-year-old boy. They played one game. The boy won, and further, had the sense to quit while he was ahead.

In this sense, backgammon differs sharply from bridge. In the game of bridge, the hand is dealt. The deal is a chance distribution of the cards. Following this, there is the chance play of the opposition. However, beyond these two factors of luck, skill rules the game. In backgammon, every move is governed first by the dice, then by the skill of the player. In addition, backgammon is one of the few games of chance and skill in which there is no concealment. The truth is naked for all to see.

Another remarkable feature of the game is that since the dawn of time, millions on millions of games have been played without a single tie. The game is structured in such a way that win or lose, you never spend time at a game which does not have an outcome. A tie cannot happen.

Adding to the excitement of the game, and presenting much the same challenge as the bidding in bridge, is the doubling factor. In bridge, one bids and then tries to make the bid. The higher the bid, the more difficult to make it, and yet the greater the reward in score if made. In backgammon, at any point in the game, if a player feels he has the advantage, he may double the stakes. Should the advantage shift, which is often the case, the opponent may then double the stakes again. The challenge of winning with the higher stakes is very stimulating to the game and to the players. There are on record instances of an entire year's winnings lost or regained in a single re-re-redoubled game.

Money! Yes, backgammon is a gambling game, played for money. It differs from the run of casino or chance games in that skill and luck are equally important. Since nobody wishes to lose money, backgammon devotees try to play their best game at every session. Players take the game very seriously.

One is never bored during a game of backgammon. Because money is involved and because the game moves like lightning, close attention is called for. There is none of the deliberation of chess, nor the seeing through of a dull hand as in bridge. If you have ever been present at a backgammon tournament, you have heard the roars of excitement and the constant clacking of dice hitting the board. Players move their men rapidly. The dice are thrown, the men are moved. Quick thinking and total concentration are necessary.

Because it is a board game, the visual excitement of watching men advance is always before you. Basically a game of running and blocking (running with all your men toward home, and blocking your opponent from doing the same), backgammon has the offensive and defensive qualities of chess. You and you alone face your opponent. There is no partner to err. If you make a bad move, you are responsible. Conversely, if you make a good move, you alone take the credit.

The fascination of backgammon also lies in its diversity. Because of the billions and billions of possible combinations of play, no two games are ever alike. And because of the doubling factor, practically a fresh start is possible with every game. Losses can be recovered and at times just one good roll of the dice can mean the difference between overwhelming victory and disastrous defeat.

Backgammon has always been a pastime of the aristocratic and the rich. In such gilded clubs as the Everglades in Palm Beach, the staid Racquet Clubs in New York and Chicago, the Metropolitan, Regency, and Racquet Clubs in Philadelphia and Boston, it has always been not only respectable but highly desirable. In the following chapter, devoted to the history of the game, you will discover that pharaohs, kings, emperors, aristocrats, and millionaires have enjoyed backgammon. On the other hand, in some sections of the world, notably the Middle East and Greece, the game has been played at all levels of society.

With this book, you will learn all that can be taught about backgammon. Beyond that, only experience will further your understanding and knowledge of the game. And after you have learned how to play, undoubtedly you will never again be the same person. For after all, you will have become a backgammon player. And that is a very special breed of humanity indeed.

Backgammon

chapter one

The Romance and History of Backgammon

An authentic, documented history of the ancient game of backgammon should probably begin either in the Garden of Eden or in the murky caves of the Neanderthal man. This is contingent upon one's commitment to either the evolutionary or divine advent of the human race. However, since the remains of the original paradise have yet to be unearthed, and since the caverns of the prehistoric creatures have to date turned up little more than a few old bones and some wall paintings, we will have to content ourselves with a mere five thousand years of backgammon history. Consider that this is the beginning of recorded history, the period when the Sumerian civilization flourished. The Sumerians predate the Babylonians and Assyrians and lived in the southern part of Mesopotamia, the ancient name for the modern country of Iraq.

During the 1920s, after a flurry of sensational archaeological discoveries, the English archaeologist Leonard Woolley started to dig in the biblical Ur of the Chaldees, the ancient home of Abraham. Several years before, important discoveries had hinted at the fact that Noah and all of his animals had existed and that the Great Deluge probably did take place right there in Sumer. Woolley excavated, all but found the ark itself, and in the meantime came up with five gaming boards which closely resemble the backgammon boards of today. It is therefore possible, if not probable, that when Noah and his sons were finished with their daily chore of feeding their floating zoo, they sat down with a glass of wine and proceeded to entertain themselves by playing backgammon.

The boards discovered in Sumer were ornately decorated with inlaid lapis lazuli, shell, red limestone, and bitumen, and illustrated with depictions of animals and rosettes. Obviously these were very special gaming boards upon which very special people played backgammon.

The year after Woolley excavated at Ur, an expedition from the University of Pennsylvania and the British Museum, digging in Mesopotamia, found more of the same. The report from the dig includes these words:

> The gaming board found in the King's grave is not so richly decorated as one found last season in Ur, but it is made more interesting by the fact that beneath it were found in neat piles the two sets of playing pieces and the dice. One set of men is composed of simple black squares inlaid with five dots each, and the other is of shell squares engraved with animal scenes. One set of dice is shell with lapis dots, the other of lapis with gold dots.

Several millenniums later, the Egyptian Pharaohs were pitting their skills in backgammon against their opponents in much the same way that the Sumerian kings had. Boards were discovered in King Tut's tomb in the Nile Valley and also as far afield as Enkomi in Cyprus, then within the realm of the Pharaohs. These date from 1500 B.C. One board discovered there, and on display in the British Museum in London, contains the cartouche of Queen Hatshepsut. Lion-headed pieces, the ancient symbol of royal power, were found with the board.

Evidently in Egypt the common people played backgammon also, for in many of the tombs there wall paintings depict people playing the game. Quite possibly it is from Egypt that the game later spread throughout the Middle East among the common people.

The Egyptians, however, had one device which does truly surpass the sophistication of the modern version of the game. This was a machine which could be called a dice box. Dice would be dropped into the machine, juggled around, and then spilled out onto the table. In this way, no cheating was possible. Obviously, the Egyptians played backgammon for money and were even more cautious about "hustling" than we are today. The Greeks and Romans later used this device in their game.

A thousand years later, backgammon was played in Greece. The game must have been very popular among the patricians of the classical civilization, for many of the intellectuals refer to it in their writings. Plato mentions backgammon and comments that it was played with great frequency by many ancient Greeks. Herodotus attributes it to the Lydians, while Sophocles mentions that the game was invented by Palamedes, who relaxed over the game with his compatriots during the siege of Troy. The game is mentioned by Homer in the Odyssey and Plutarch, a later Greek writer, even goes so far as to say that "Mercury once played at dice with the moon."

The ancient Greeks must have reacted emotionally to good and bad rolls in a similar manner to the reaction of contemporary players. Sixes, which were high, were referred to as "Aphrodite," and ones, which were low, were called the Greek equivalent of "dog."

After the Greeks were superseded by the Romans as leaders of the Western world, backgammon continued to be the most popular of games among the ruling class. It was regarded as the sport of the emperors, and rivaled the

Circus Maximus and the Colosseum as a leisure pastime. One Roman emperor even went so far as to have a special room set aside for dicing. The Emperor Claudius wrote a book on the subject. It is known that the Emperor Domitian was an expert player and that Caligula was a cheat. No different from the reputations which some players hold in backgammon circles today.

Everybody knows that Antony risked an empire to remain in Egypt, but few know that he played at Ludus Duodecim Scriptorum (the Roman name for backgammon) with Cleopatra.

Evidently the Romans often added the spice of sex to their game. An early version of "strip poker" is depicted on the back of an ancient, silver looking glass. A young patrician and a young maid sit partially undressed in front of a backgammon board. A few pieces of clothing lie on the floor nearby. The inscription reads "Devincamted," which translated means, "I believe I have beaten you." What came next is anyone's guess.

During the decadence of the later Roman Empire, the game became even more popular. Nero is said to have played for as much as $15,000 a point. Lampridius mentions that Commodus virtually turned the Imperial Palace into a gambling den. At one point during his reign, he apparently was in financial need. He went to the treasury and claimed he was about to go to visit the African provinces and would need financing. The money was granted, and he promptly went back to the backgammon tables and lost every cent of it.

The game evidently sifted down to the man in the street, as wall paintings in Pompeii depict a backgammon incident. In one panel, a game is in process and an argument has ensued over points. In the second, an innkeeper is throwing the two battling players out of his tavern. To this day, backgammon still provokes heated disagreement.

The Romans seemed to have had a sense of humor about the game, for a table found in Rome is inscribed with the following words:

IDIOTA   RECEDE

This translated means:

IDIOT   GET OUT

At the beginning of the Christian era in Rome, backgammon continued to be played. In fact, the new savior was even called upon for assistance. Among the Christian antiquities in Rome, there is a marble slab on which is cut a backgammon board. A Greek cross is in the center and the inscription reads: "Jesus Christ gives victory and help to dicers if they write his name when they throw the dice, Amen."

During this period, the game of tabula, a variation of the earlier Roman game, became popular. In fact, tabula was so universally played in Rome that a remarkable defeat suffered by the Emperor Zeno has been completely documented, move for move. Several renditions of the entire board at the time of his disastrous throw have survived the ages.

From Rome, the game spread throughout the Empire. George Frederick Pardon, in his book *Backgammon: Its History and Practice,* published in London in 1844, says:

> That it differed from our game may be admitted, but it was played with the same number of partly colored counters, by two alternate players with dice, on tables with the same number of lines as ours, and it possessed the same happy admixture of chance and skill.

It is probable that the Romans brought the game with them when they invaded Britain and that it gradually evolved into the game it is today.

During the first millennium after Christ, backgammon was played throughout the Middle East. Whether or not the Romans were responsible for its popularization or if it just continued to be played after Sumer crumbled is not known. However, in the *Journal of the Asiatic Society of Bengal,* H. G. Raverty, in an article entitled "The Invention of Chess and Backgammon," writes:

> Ard-shir Babakan, son of Babak of the Sasanian dynasty of Iran-Zamin or the ancient Persian Empire, invented it. The game was also sometimes called Nard-i-shir after him.

Mr. Raverty goes on to explain that the game was played on a checkered cloth which folded up and that it contained twelve divisions according to the solar months of the Persian year. The muhrahs or counters with which Nard was played corresponded with the number of days of the lunar month of the fire worshipers or ancient Persians. Half of the counters were white, the other half black, because on half of the month there were moonlit nights and on the other half dark ones. The moves from one division or space to another, Ard-shir Babakan likened to the decrees of destiny, which vary and change, are turned and inverted, in the life of every human being. The fact of each one differs from the fact of another.

The names of the seven points in Nard were called Kad, which means quantity; Ziyad, which means increase or growth; Satarah, which means veil, curtain, star, or fortune; Hazaran, thousands; Khanah-gir, holder or possessor of the house or compartment; Tawil, long, prolix, or tall; and Mansubah, plan, project, scheme, or game.

Backgammon, however, was not only played in the centers of the traditional sweep of Western history. It is known that the game found its way to Japan by way of India and China.

Obviously, this game is vastly different from today's standard backgammon; however, the derivation appears to be the same.

Throughout the Middle Ages, backgammon continued to flourish and proliferate. Artisans created highly ornate boards which eventually even found their way into church decoration. Medieval cathedrals in Germany often contain representations of backgammon boards. Illuminated manuscripts were created explaining and illustrating the game.

The English in particular seemed to latch onto backgammon with great fervor. It was known first as "tables," obviously derived from the Latin "tabula" which the Romans brought with them during the invasion. English literature is full of allusions to the game. Chaucer refers to it in *Canterbury Tales* and says, "They dancen and they play at ches and tables." Spenser refers to it in *The Faerie Queene*. Bacon says, "Dice and cards may sometimes be used for recreation when field sports cannot be had." Addison and Dryden mention it as a gentlemanly pastime and one writer says, "It is an anodyne to the gout, the rheumatism, the azure devils or the yellow spleen."

Another writer says in praise of the game, "From time immemorial, backgammon has held the foremost position among the elite of popular games. It has ever been a game for the higher classes and has never been vulgarized or defiled by uneducated people. In that respect it differs from whist (father of our contract bridge), which has seen its day in the servants' hall, but will ever be shunned in higher circles."

Swift once advised a country friend to study the game, "that he might be on friendly, that is on playing terms with the rector." He added, "And certainly debates about hits were easier of settlement than disputes about tithes from Sir Roger de Coverley, when he wished to obtain from the University a chaplain of piety and urbanity, in short a Christian minister, conditioned that he should know something about backgammon."

Soame Jenyns in 1735 wrote:

> Here you'll be ever sure to meet
> A hearty welcome, though no treat;
> A house, where quiet guards the door,
> No rural wits smoke, drink and roar;
> Choice books, safe horses, wholesome liquor
> Billiards, backgammon and the vicar.

Obviously backgammon was always equated with the good life in England. During the mid-nineteenth century, George Frederick Pardon wrote of backgammon:

Our honored patrons, the public were pleased to receive very graciously a former work of ours. We are induced therefore, to present unto them another and the ceremony of the presentation requires a Preface.

We catered, in the first instance, for social amusement, for the gratification of a quadrangular party, we now seek to please the smallest party, but the tenderest number . . . the gentle dual number to which the Greek tongue only has done justice . . . two; not partners, but in closer contact . . . not with identical interests

17

in the game, but frequently with assimilated affections in life . . . not fearful of playing wrongs, because responsible to an expecting and much expectant co-mate, but causing good humour by bad play, a hearty laugh for a thoughtless move. Let all who enjoy this recreation . . . the lover, the husband, the grandiose, the happy maiden and the happier wife . . . all who have pleasant leisure or peaceful evenings, yield us their approbation, and we will defy criticism as boldly as Hamlet augury.

Never feeleth man more grateful to his household gods than when he converseth cheerily of past days, with his helpmate by his old hearth, or doth contend with her at tables, which many do call backgammon and which, will I . . . should be the sole contention persevered in them between "ancient authors."

In the past, some backgammon boards were bound as books. Here is one with a fairly lettered outside which might impose upon the uninitiated; it is like a shallow pendant . . . has a learned air, but no lore within; it is entitled, "The History of England, Vol. I and Vol. II." And to do it justice may be called an emblematical history; open it and what are the contents? Men of two parties, dice and boxes; men and the means of combat. What better epitome can there be of history? Is it at one long and little, varied tale of struggles between two parties, desperate efforts to push opponents from their vantage ground . . . struggles in which genius and skill do not always avail unless with the aid of chance; a picture of difficulties, reverses, captures, revolutions? Backgammon embodies all these things.

The technical terms of backgammon may teach us valuable lessons. In the game, it is proper to get your men to your table and to effect it as rapidly as possible; that teaches hospitality, brisk as its own champagne. "Cover your man" is another maxim; that shows protection must be afforded to the helpless, clothing to him whose "looped and windowed raggedness' demands payment of such charitable impost; tis moreover to diminish the amount of poor's rate, by encouraging manufactures, and let political economists prescribe a better remedy. Get home as quickly as you can inculcates the culture of domestic happiness . . . suggests a speedy return from even the most festive scenes in order to light up eyes that such return renders brighter than the tapers by which the loved one waits and muses. . . . "Go back" is often said at backgammon, and should be the endeavor of the wanderer from the path of rectitude ere the second false step has been taken. After that, facilis descensus Averni, he will find returning more difficult than the Chinese language.

In English history there are several significant records mentioning backgammon. It is known that James I of Scotland spent the last evening of his life, the one prior to his murder in the Abbey of the Black Friars at Perth in 1437, in "reading with his queen and with the nobles and ladies of his court and in playing at tables and chess."

It is also known that, in 1479, when the Duke of Albany, the brother of James III, was confined in Edinburgh Castle, he "one evening invited the captain of the guard to sup with him; the evening was spent in hilarity, in playing at tables. And in the morning, the royal prisoner had escaped, and his gaoler, guest, lay a blackened corpse upon the hearth."

The Romance and History of Backgammon

Richard the Lion-Hearted and Philip Augustus of France prohibited anyone in the army of the Crusaders under the degree of a knight from playing at this or other games for money. There was a scale for the knights, nobles, and prelates, beyond which they might not play, while the kings themselves were unlimited in their stakes.

So we see that backgammon has always been considered the "right" game for everyone from kings to even higher functionaries of the church.

In the United States it has been played since the earliest days of our history. However, perhaps the most amusing and significant anecdote concerns Thomas Jefferson. On June 10, 1776, the Continental Congress appointed the distinguished gentleman from Virignia to draft the Declaration of Independence, issued on July 4 of that year. What did Jefferson do for relaxation during that period? Among surviving records is a notebook of expenses which he kept for the three weeks. Two entries during the period read: "Lost at backgammon 7/6. Won at backgammon 7d/1/3."

Exactly how backgammon came to be played in pre-Colombian Mexico is unknown. But the discovery of boards and the documentation of games played written by early Spanish writers help to substantiate the fact that the Indian civilizations of the Western Hemisphere probably came from Asia, where a similar game was played.

In the writings of Francisco López de Gomara in 1552, a year after the Spanish conquest, the game is mentioned:

Sometimes Montezuma looked on as they played patolli, which much resembles the game of tables. It is played with beans, marked like one-faced dice, which they call patolli. They take them between the hands and throw them on a mat or table or on the ground, where there are certain lines like a merel (or a draught board) on which they mark like stones the point which fell up, taking off and putting on a little stone.

In his *Monarquía Indiana* (1616) Juan de Torquemada presents even more details, including a diagram of the board and a description of the places.

Evidently the game ceased to be played in Mexico shortly after the conquest, as it was equated with some superstitious belief in connection with the conquest.

Further, the primitive Iroquois Indians played a game called "Gus-ka-eh" with a bowl and peach stones. The people believed that they would continue playing this game in their afterlife. It was a betting game, in which the players were divided by tribes, and was always introduced as the final exercise at the Green Corn Harvest Festival and also at the New Year's Jubilee.

Backgammon has always been played everywhere. The game has always been a gentleman's game. During the nineteenth century, the English played it feverishly in their clubs. And during the late nineteenth century, Americans in their quest for association with the "lord of the manor" adopted the game as their own. It has since been played in most of the private clubs in our cities and in our more exclusive resorts. And as leisure increases here and abroad more and more people are finding this game of skill and chance an exciting and gratifying way to relax. Backgammon, the king of games, the game of kings, is being discovered by everybody.

chapter two

The Basics

Now that you have been acquainted with the fascinating history and romance of the game of backgammon, it is time to learn how to play. Backgammon boards are available in a wide range of styles varying in price from a few dollars to literally thousands for antique, inlaid ivory and wood, lapis, or lacquered boards.

I. THE EQUIPMENT OF THE GAME

15 Black men

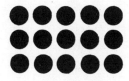

15 White men

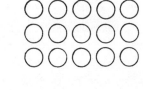

Two dice cups. These should have a shallow lip inside the cup. The lip serves to thwart attempts by dishonest dice rollers to fix the combinations on the dice. This is not to assume that backgammon players are dishonest; however, in this day and age, as always, one can never be too cautious.

Backgammon

One doubling block, sometimes called doubling cube.

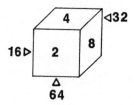

One backgammon board.

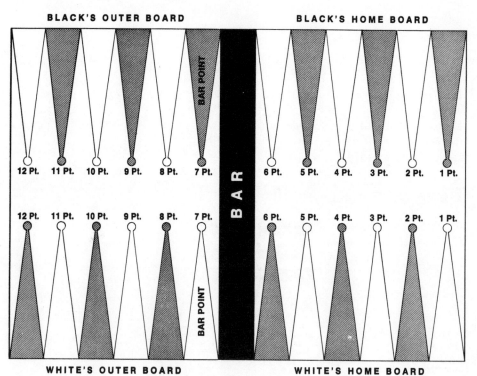

You will notice that the backgammon board is divided into four sections, a home board and an outer board for each player. In some circles the term "table" is used instead of board. "Board," however, is the preferred word today and will be used consistently in this book. In addition, the term "inner" is sometimes used instead of "home." But again, "home" will be used consistently in this book.

Each of the four boards contains six long, narrow, triangular-shaped spaces. The reason why they are triangular in shape is that points of triangles are relatively easy to count. These "points," as they are called, alternate in contrasting colors to further facilitate rapid counting. As you learn the game and the basic process of moving your men from point to point according to the throws of the dice, you will become adept at rapidly counting these points. Celerity makes for a more exciting game, and all good players play a fast game.

Notice that on the illustration the home board on each side is numbered from one to six, with the outer board numbered from seven to twelve, for a sum total of twenty-four points. The game is played by moving the men from point to point according to the number rolled on the dice.

The points are not actually numbered on standard boards, nor are the home and outer boards labeled. However, you must, upon learning the game, commit these to memory immediately. Each of the points is long enough to hold five men, with spare room for a sixth. The space between the ends of the points on the two opposing sides of the board should be wide enough for the players to throw the dice.

As you will note in the illustration, the center of the board is disected by a "bar." This is the dividing space between the home and outer boards. The purpose of the bar is to facilitate counting the points when you move your men. Six points lie to the right of the bar and six to the left. The bar is also the place where men who have been "hit" or "knocked off" are placed. This will be explained later in this chapter.

The point directly to the left of the bar, just outside of White's home board, the seven-point, is called the "bar point." From Black's side of the board, the bar point lies to the right of the bar. If you are a beginner at the game, solidly grasp this information by thoroughly studying the diagram. The seven-point will be referred to as the bar point throughout the rest of the book.

II. THE SETUP OF THE GAME

The men are placed on the four boards: Black's home board, Black's outer board, White's home board, and White's outer board, according to the illustrations. As you will notice, there are two ways to set up the board. It is strongly recommended that you accustom yourself to setting up the board in both ways. The two methods evolved many years before modern lighting was invented, for the sole purpose of facilitating bearing off men. "Bearing off" will be explained later in this chapter. The home board was always placed nearest the source of light. Today, the use of the two setups is simply a matter of habit and etiquette. There is *no* other significance in using them.

The first setup illustrated will be used consistently throughout the book for instruction.

Through the evolution of the game and according to the present custom, both players agree as to which way the board will be set up before the game begins. There is *no* strategic advantage afforded one player or the other in either of the two setups.

Backgammon

The first setup.

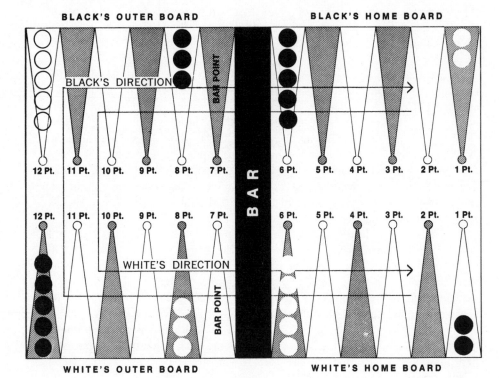

White's men are located as follows:
2 men on Black's one-point;
5 men on Black's twelve-point;
3 men on White's eight-point;
5 men on White's six-point.

Black's men are located as follows:
2 men on White's one-point;
5 men on White's twelve-point;
3 men on Black's eight-point;
5 men on Black's six-point.

The second setup.

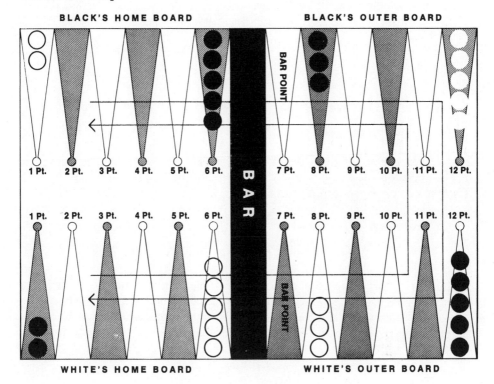

White's men are located as follows:

2 men on Black's one-point;
5 men on Black's twelve-point;
3 men on White's eight-point;
5 men on White's six-point.

Black's men are located as follows:

2 men on White's one-point;
5 men on White's twelve-point;
5 men on Black's six-point;
3 men on Black's eight-point.

To reiterate, learn both methods of setting up the board for play. Do *not* accustom yourself to one setup only!

III. THE OBJECT OF THE GAME

To win you must do two things:

1. Move all your men to your home board. When that is done and not before,

2. Bear off all your men. The first person completing these tasks wins the game.

IV. HOW THE GAME IS PLAYED

A. Starting the game

Each player rolls one die. The high roller moves first and he moves the combination shown on the two dice. If there is a tie, throw again. After the first throw, players throw alternately.

B. Moving

If the throw is not a double, the player moves what the dice indicate individually, not in sum total as in a crap game. A 4/6 is four-six or six-four, not ten. A throw of 4/6 allows a move of one man four points and a second man six points. Or the move of one man first four and then six points.

If the throw is a double, the player is entitled to double the value of the double in moves. Thus double threes can be played in any of the following ways:

1. Any four men may be moved three points each.

2. Any one man may be moved twelve points.

3. Any two men may be moved six points each.

4. Any one man may be moved nine points, and any one man three points.

5. Any two men may be moved three points each, and any one man may be moved six points.

C. Occupying spaces and hitting

1. If a space is unoccupied, either player may occupy it.

2. If a space has only one man on it, the man is vulnerable (defined as a "blot"). If the opponent makes a throw that lands one or more of his men on a blot, the man is sent off the board. This is called a "hit." The man must then re-enter and begin again.

3. If a space has two or more men on it, the men are secure from attack and cannot be hit. Such a space is called a "point."

4. A space can only have men of one color on it at a time. When a hit takes place, the newcomer usurps the tenant; they do not coexist on the space.

5. Points of either color may be counted over as though they did not exist. However, the places where you touch down during the count must not be

occupied by an opponent's point. You can land on: (a) your own point; (b) an open space; (c) your own blot; (d) your opponent's blot (hitting him); but *not* on your opponent's point.

NOTE ON MOVING AND OCCUPYING SPACES

When moving one man more than once in a roll, you are assumed to come to rest on the spaces indicated on the dice. For example, if you throw 3/6 and space nine is vacant but the spaces three away and six away are blocked by opponent's points, you cannot move that one man nine spaces.

Continuing the example, suppose you next rolled 4/5 with point five away open and point four away blocked. You could make this move not by counting four and then five, but by counting five and then four. See illustration.

It is White's move. He has rolled a 6/3.

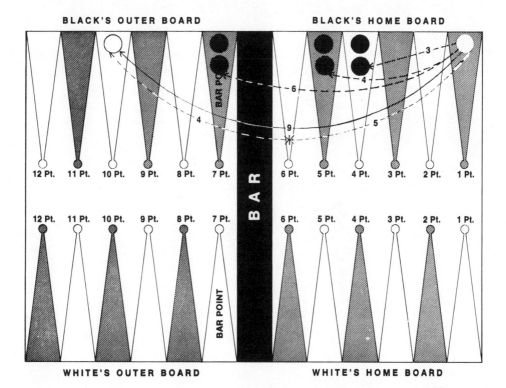

BLACK'S OUTER BOARD   BLACK'S HOME BOARD

| 12 Pt. | 11 Pt. | 10 Pt. | 9 Pt. | 8 Pt. | 7 Pt. | 6 Pt. | 5 Pt. | 4 Pt. | 3 Pt. | 2 Pt. | 1 Pt. |

BAR POINT

WHITE'S OUTER BOARD   WHITE'S HOME BOARD

White cannot move three, then six, because three points away from where he is is blocked. He cannot move six, then three, because six points away from where he is is blocked. Therefore, he cannot move this man 6/3.

If, on the other hand, White had rolled 5/4, he could not move four, then five, because four points away from where he is is blocked, but he *could* move five, then four, because point five away is open. He therefore can move this man 5/4.

D. Re-entering

If hit, a man is sent off the board (to the rail, to the bar, back home). If a player has one or more men on the rail he can make no other play until he gets them back on the board.

You must re-enter in your opponent's home board. To do this, you must throw on *one of the two dice* a number of a space not blocked by an opponent's point. Thus if early in the game the opponent has only the six-point blocked, then either a one, two, three, four, or five will do. If late in the game only the two-point is open, then you must keep throwing until you roll a two. If the board is entirely closed, (the ultimate defensive situation) you need not shake at all, for there is no space for you to re-enter on.

NOTE ON RE-ENTERING

Remember you cannot come in onto a point blocked by your opponent. You can come in on: (a) a vacant space; (b) a point which you possess in your opponent's home board; (c) your own blot in his home board; (d) and even on your opponent's blot—this is a hit like any other and puts his man off the board, in the same fix you have just been in. Naturally he must re-enter in your home board.

White wishes to re-enter.

BLACK'S HOME BOARD

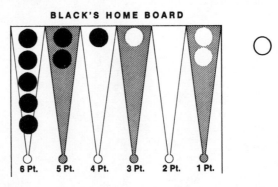

White cannot come in on six or five, because these points are blocked by Black.

White can come in on one because he has two men on the one-point.

White can come in on two because the two-point is open.

White can come in on three because he has a man on the three-point.

White can come in on four, *and hit Black,* sending him off the board.

E. Ending the game

Remember, first all fifteen men must be moved into the home board. (Note that you begin the game with five of them already there.) When, and only when, this is accomplished, you may begin to bear off. The game ends when one player has borne off his last man, to become the winner.

F. Rules for bearing off

Visualize the points in your home board numbered from one to six.

1. If your throw is not a double, you may remove one of your men from each point indicated on the dice. Thus a 4/2 allows you to remove one man from the four-point and one man from the two-point.

2. If your throw is a double, as always you are entitled to double the value of the double. Thus double five entitles you to remove four men from the five-point.

3. If you have no men on the six-point and you throw a six on one die, you can take a man off the highest point on which you do have men as though it were a six. Similarly, if you have no men on the six- or five-points and you roll a six or a five, you can take off the highest man. And so on down the line. Generally stated, when you throw a number larger than the highest point on which you have a man, a man from the highest point may be borne off.

The rule applies with doubles too. E.g., assume you had two men on the five-point and one man each on the two-point and three-point. A shake of double five could take them all off. The first two fives off leaves the three the highest occupied point. So you can take this man off. This leaves the two the highest point, so you can bear it off to make the fourth five of the double five.

4. You do not have to bear off if you can and wish to move inside the home board. You must use the entire roll if possible, but you may bear off two men, or move two inside, or bear one off and move one. This becomes particularly important when the opponent has one or more points in your home board trying for a last-ditch shot at you.

5. If you are hit while bearing off, you must re-enter as usual and get the stray man back into the home board before you can recommence bearing off.

G. Winning the game

There are three degrees of victory:

1. The regular "win," where the loser has borne off at least one man. The victor wins the amount at stake.

2. The "gammon," where the loser has *not* borne off at least one man. The victor wins double the stake.

3. The "backgammon," where the loser has not borne off at least one man and has one or more men stranded in the winner's home board or on the rail. The victor wins three times the stake.

chapter three

The First Move

Throughout the thousands of years that backgammon has been played, a series of the most advantageous first moves has evolved. These are considered basic to the game. You will discover as you read this chapter that some rolls of the dice are decidedly advantageous, while others are not. Some will lead to a running situation, others to a defensive blocking strategy. Some call for cautious playing, others for aggressive, daring play. Master all of these thoroughly.

Exceptions, of course, exist, depending on special situations. These will be discussed later, in the chapter on psychology.

In the following examples, to open the game each player rolls one die, then the player with the higher die moves first, moving the combination of the two dice. If there is a tie, each throws the dice again.

To fully grasp the basic instructions in this chapter and the following one, the board must be set up appropriately. In each of the following, assume that White moves first.

THE TWO AND ONE MOVE

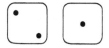

White moves one man from Black's one-point to Black's two-point, and one man from Black's twelve-point to his own eleven-point.

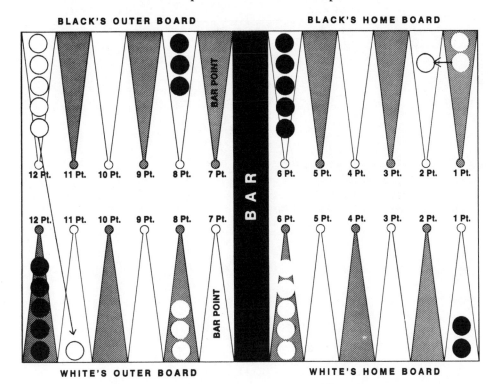

LOGIC: White is immediately putting into effect the object of the game, that is, "running" and "blocking." (Running and blocking games will be explained in future chapters.) Although generally the 2/1 roll is not considered a good roll, moving the two to his own eleven-point gives White what is known as a "builder." A builder is a man brought down close to your home board as an extra man. With him, you may hope to make an additional point in your home board or just outside your home board.

When White moves more of his men to this point, he will be able to block his opponent from getting out of his home board. At the same time, moving the one starts White running.

31

ALTERNATIVE TWO AND ONE MOVE

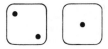

White moves one man from Black's twelve-point to his own eleven-point, and one man from his own six-point to his five-point.

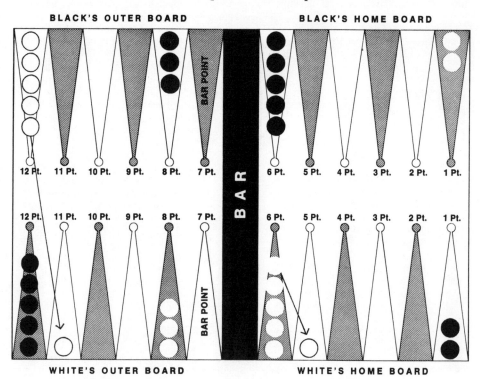

LOGIC: This move is considered by some as making the best of a bad roll. If Black does not hit White and he can cover his blots on his next roll, White will have a nice advantage. If not, and one or both opening men get sent home, it is time for him to play a back game. (Back games will be explained in a future chapter.)

THE THREE AND ONE MOVE

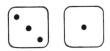

White moves one man from his eight-point to his five-point, and one man from his six-point to his five-point.

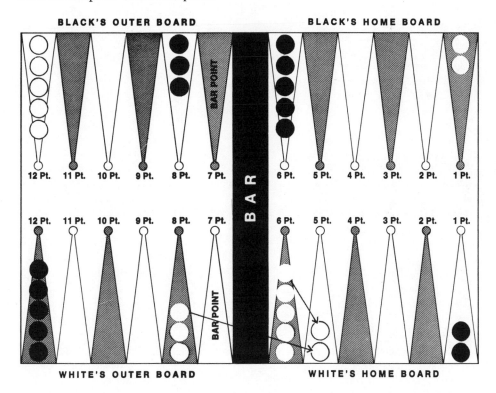

LOGIC: This is a good roll. The player has made a point on his five-point, considered the most important on his home board, and has created an additional block against his opponent.

THE FOUR AND TWO MOVE

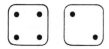

White moves one man from his eight-point to his four-point, and one man from his six-point to his four-point.

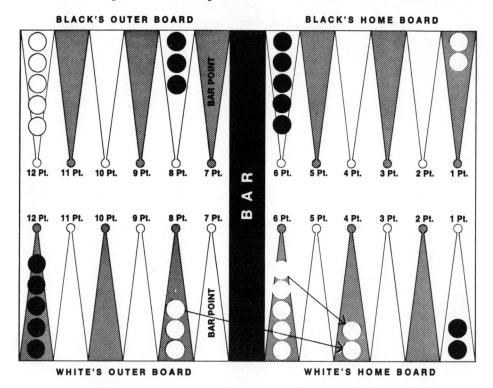

LOGIC: This is a good roll. Here again, the player has made a point on his home board and has created an additional block against his opponent.

THE FIVE AND THREE MOVE

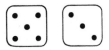

White moves one man from his eight-point to his three-point, and one man from his six-point to his three-point.

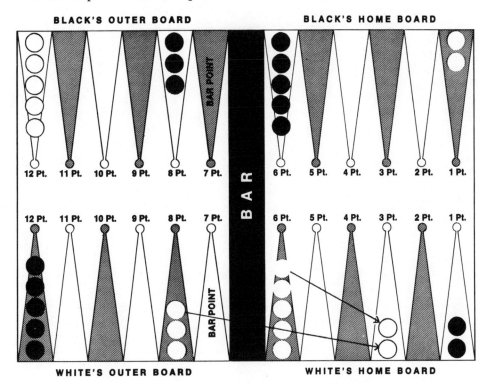

LOGIC: This is also a good roll. And, again, the player has made a point on his home board and has created an additional block against his opponent.

ALTERNATIVE FIVE AND THREE MOVE

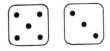

White moves one man from Black's twelve-point to his own ten-point, and one man from Black's twelve-point to his own eight-point.

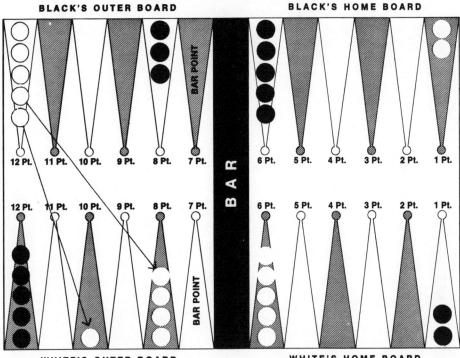

BLACK'S OUTER BOARD **BLACK'S HOME BOARD**

| 12 Pt. | 11 Pt. | 10 Pt. | 9 Pt. | 8 Pt. | 7 Pt. | | 6 Pt. | 5 Pt. | 4 Pt. | 3 Pt. | 2 Pt. | 1 Pt. |

BAR POINT

B A R

| 12 Pt. | 11 Pt. | 10 Pt. | 9 Pt. | 8 Pt. | 7 Pt. | | 6 Pt. | 5 Pt. | 4 Pt. | 3 Pt. | 2 Pt. | 1 Pt. |

BAR POINT

WHITE'S OUTER BOARD **WHITE'S HOME BOARD**

LOGIC: This move implies taking chances early in the game. It also affords a builder for closing the bar point or the five-point. It is considered by aggressive players as a better move than making a point on White's three-point.

THE FOUR AND ONE MOVE

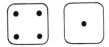

White moves one man from Black's twelve-point to his own nine-point, and one man from Black's one-point to Black's two-point.

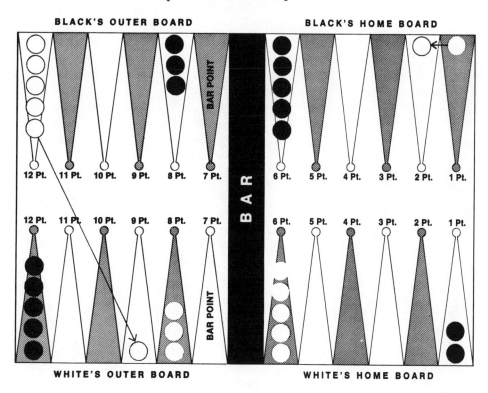

LOGIC: The same logic applies here as in the two and one move. However, here White is establishing a builder and starting to run with his back men.

ALTERNATIVE FOUR AND ONE MOVE

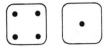

White moves one man from Black's twelve-point to his own nine-point, and one man from his own six-point to his five-point.

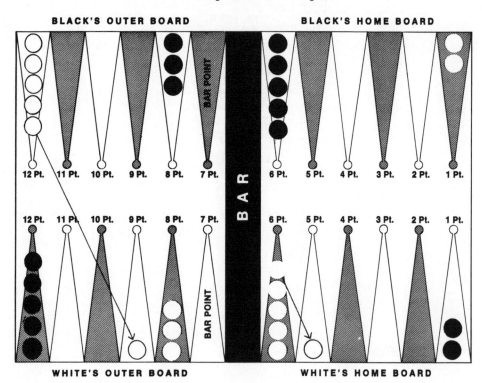

LOGIC: The logic is the same here as for the alternative two and one move.

THE FIVE AND ONE MOVE

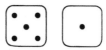

White moves one man from Black's one-point to Black's two-point, and one man from Black's twelve-point to his own eight-point.

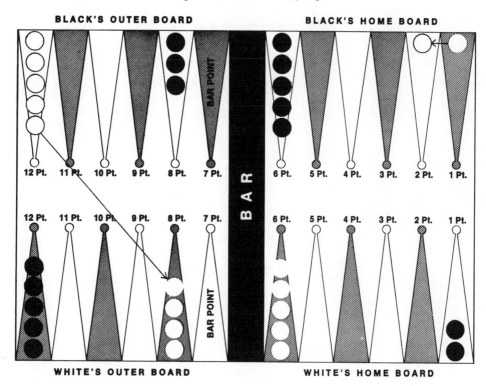

LOGIC: This is not considered a good roll. The only thing this move accomplishes is to start the game.

ALTERNATIVE FIVE AND ONE MOVE

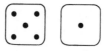

White moves one man from Black's one-point to Black's bar point.

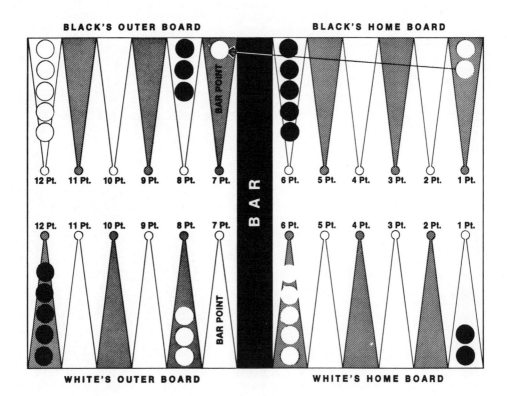

LOGIC: This is not a good move. The purpose of playing it this way is two-fold. First, White is putting out bait to be hit on Black's bar point. If he is hit, he in turn can hit Black when coming in with a combined roll of seven or a combination roll with one die reading six. Black would then have two men on White's home board. And one man waiting to get back into the game.

THE SIX AND ONE MOVE

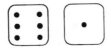

White moves one man from Black's twelve-point to his own bar point, and one man from his own eight-point to his bar point.

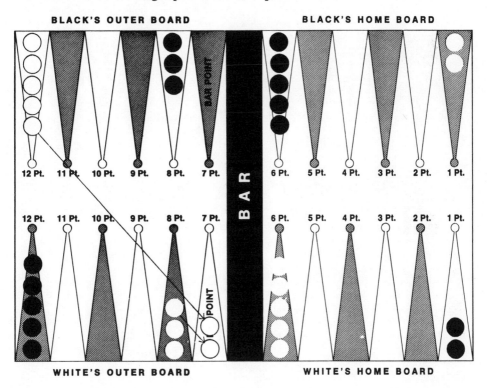

BLACK'S OUTER BOARD   **BLACK'S HOME BOARD**

WHITE'S OUTER BOARD   **WHITE'S HOME BOARD**

LOGIC: This is considered one of the best opening rolls. It can easily be seen that White now has a block of three points in a row.

THE THREE AND TWO MOVE

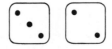

White moves one man from Black's twelve-point to his own eleven-point, and one man from Black's twelve-point to his own ten-point.

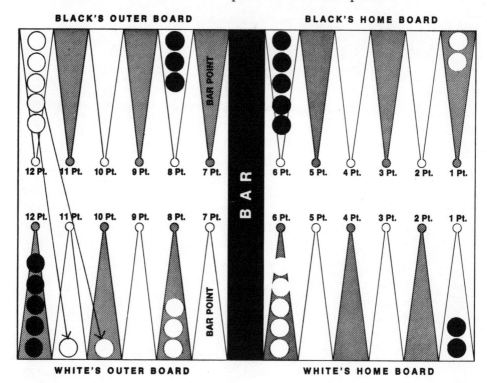

LOGIC: This is a fair roll. White is getting two men out as builders to block his opponent from getting out of his home board. He has five different positions from which he may make points on his home board, thus keeping his opponent bottled up. This is important.

THE FIVE AND TWO MOVE

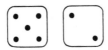

White moves one man from Black's twelve-point to his own eleven-point, and one man from Black's twelve-point to his own eight-point.

BLACK'S OUTER BOARD   **BLACK'S HOME BOARD**

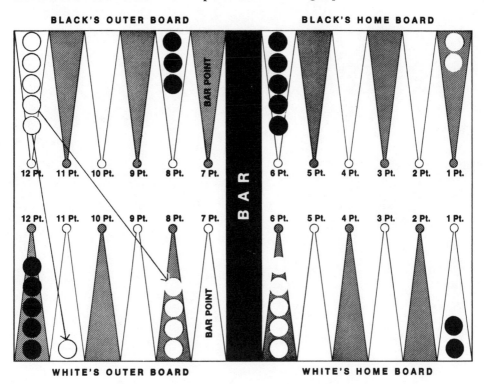

WHITE'S OUTER BOARD   **WHITE'S HOME BOARD**

LOGIC: This is a fair roll. The play is strictly in anticipation of a blocking move. Even though this does not follow the blocking-running theory, it is obvious that although you could play a two from Black's one-point to Black's three-point, this move would not advance your man very far on Black's home board.

THE SIX AND TWO MOVE

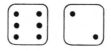

White moves one man from Black's one-point to Black's bar point, and then to Black's nine-point for a total of eight.

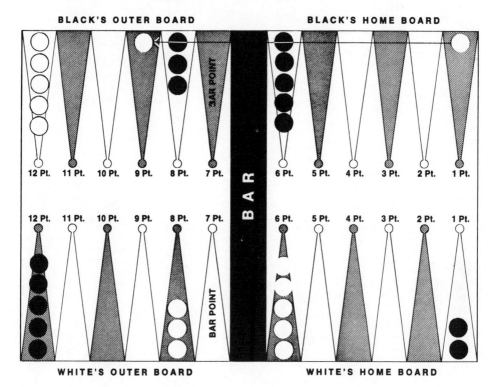

LOGIC: This is considered a bad roll. Whereas the five and two was a blocking play, this is a running play, simply making the best of a bad situation.

ALTERNATIVE SIX AND TWO MOVE—*A*

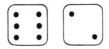

White moves one man from Black's twelve-point to his own five-point.

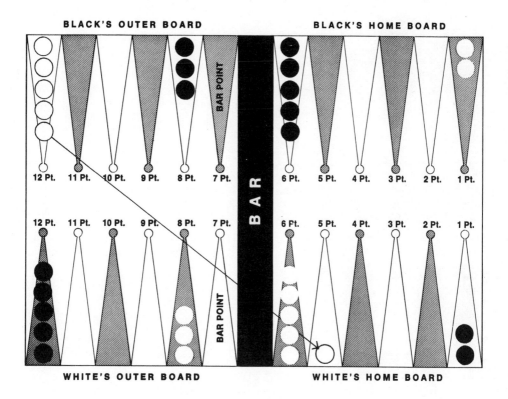

LOGIC: This is not a good move. If White does not get hit on Black's next roll, White should be able to cover his five-point.

ALTERNATIVE SIX AND TWO MOVE—*B*

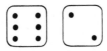

White moves one man from Black's one-point to Black's bar point, and one man from Black's twelve-point to his own eleven-point.

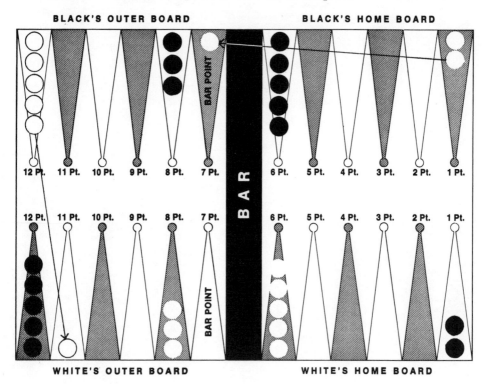

LOGIC: Same as for the alternative five and one move.

THE FOUR AND THREE MOVE

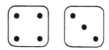

White moves one man from Black's one-point to Black's five-point, and one man from Black's twelve point to his own ten-point.

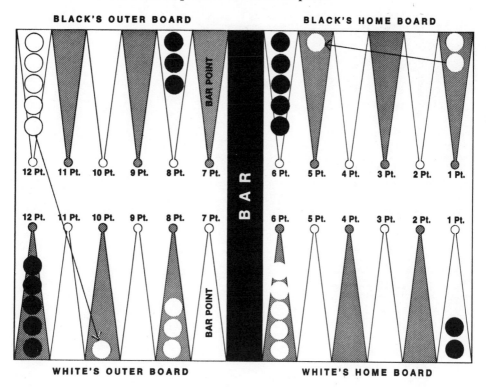

LOGIC: This is considered a fair roll. It accomplishes positioning for running and blocking.

Backgammon

ALTERNATIVE FOUR AND THREE MOVE

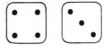

White moves one man from Black's twelve-point to his own ten-point, and one man from Black's twelve-point to his own nine-point.

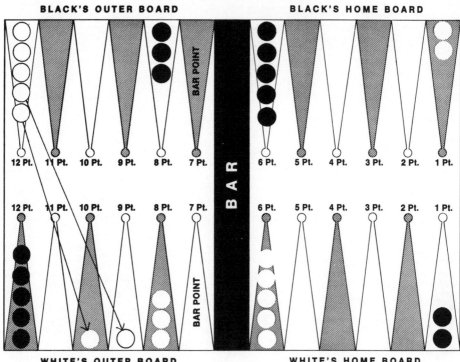

LOGIC: Here, as in the alternative three and two move, White gets two additional men out as builders to block his opponent's escape from his home board.

THE SIX AND THREE MOVE

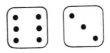

White moves one man from Black's one-point to Black's ten-point.

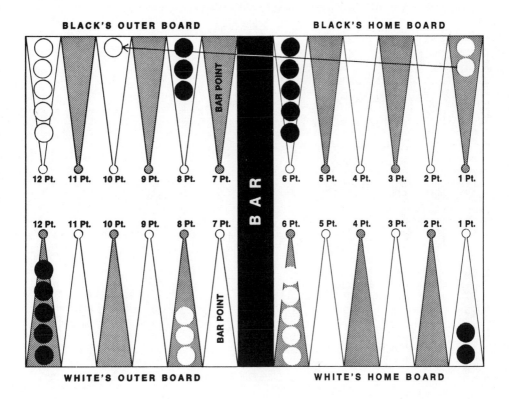

LOGIC: This is considered a bad roll. Only running is accomplished.

ALTERNATIVE SIX AND THREE MOVE

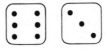

White moves one man from Black's one-point to Black's bar point, and one man from Black's twelve-point to his own ten-point.

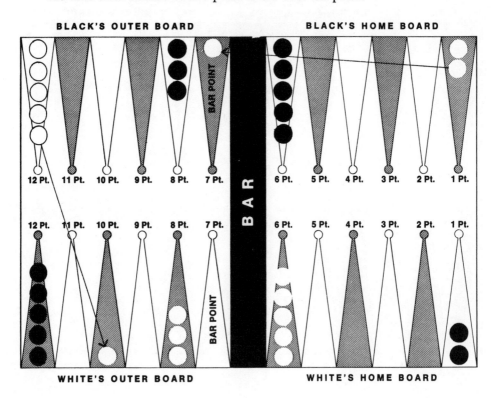

LOGIC: Same as for alternative five and one move.

THE FIVE AND FOUR MOVE

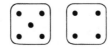

White moves one man from Black's one-point to Black's five-point, and one man from Black's twelve-point to his own eight-point.

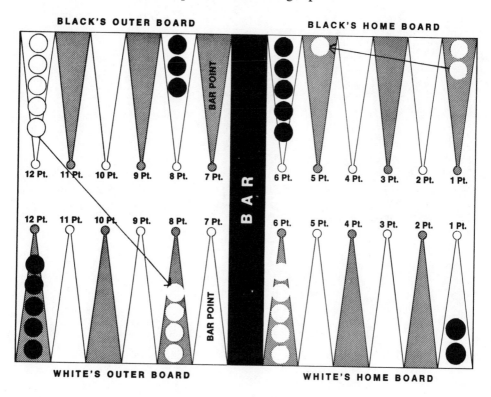

LOGIC: This is a fair roll. It accomplishes running and blocking.

THE SIX AND FOUR MOVE

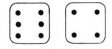

White moves one man from Black's one-point to Black's eleven-point.

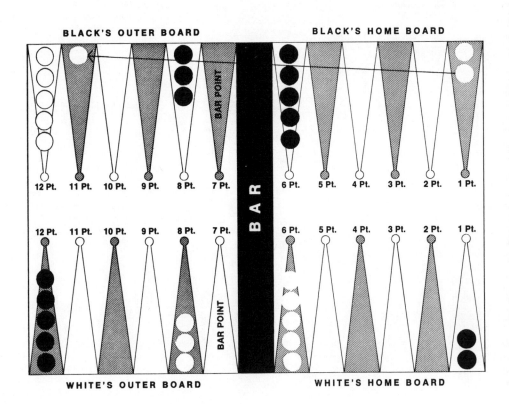

LOGIC: This is considered a bad roll. The above is a running play.

ALTERNATIVE SIX AND FOUR MOVE

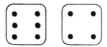

White moves one man from his eight-point to his two-point, and one man from his six-point to his two-point.

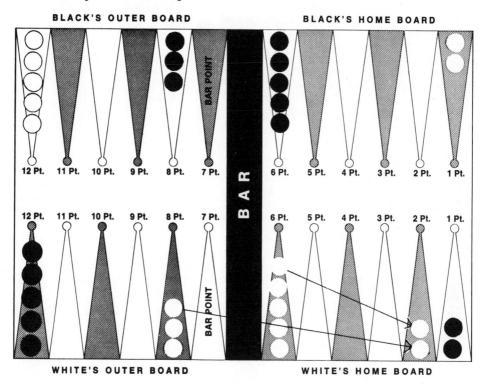

LOGIC: This play will make an additional point on White's home board. However, it creates a large gap between White's points and is not recommended.

THE SIX AND FIVE MOVE

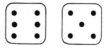

White moves one man from Black's one-point to Black's twelve-point.

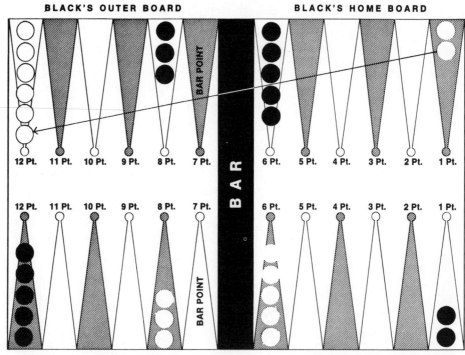

LOGIC: This is an excellent roll for a running play. White has brought one man a long way to safety. Should White roll a second six and five, his advantage will increase tremendously. In a recent experiment, twenty-one games were played with a six and five opening. The player won sixteen of the twenty-one games.

In backgammon parlance, the move is known as "lover's leap." A student of backgammon recently replied upon being asked if she had mastered the move, "I'll never forget the 'bride's slide.' "

DOUBLES

When a player rolls doubles, that is, the same number on each die, he receives a bonus and moves double the total of the dice. All opening doubles are excellent rolls except double fives.

The double opening play is rolled by the second player, after the preceding moves have been made.

DOUBLE ONES

Assuming that Black opened, White moves two men from his own eight-point to his bar point, and two men from his six-point to his five-point.

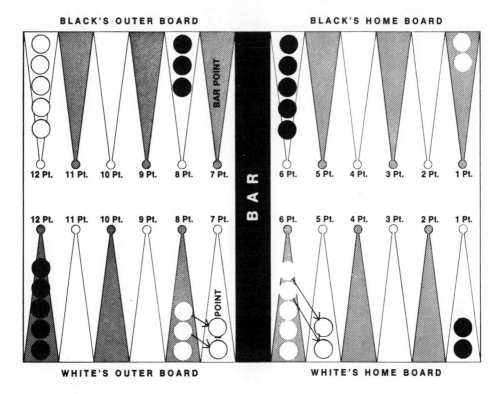

BLACK'S OUTER BOARD   BLACK'S HOME BOARD

WHITE'S OUTER BOARD   WHITE'S HOME BOARD

LOGIC: This is an excellent roll, with this particular move the best blocking opening move in backgammon. White immediately establishes a three-point consecutive block, needing only a five (from Black's twelve-point to White's eight-point) on his next roll to establish a four-point block.

DOUBLE TWOS

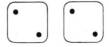

Assuming that Black opened, White moves two men from Black's twelve-point to his own eleven-point, and two men from his six-point to his four-point.

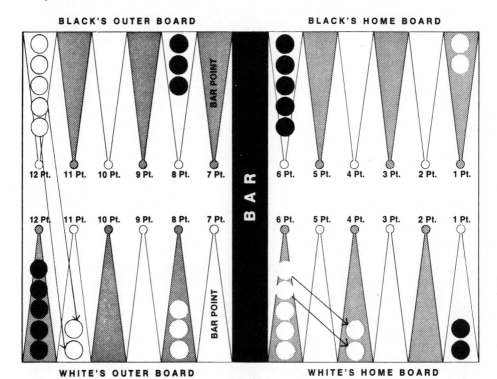

BLACK'S OUTER BOARD   **BLACK'S HOME BOARD**

WHITE'S OUTER BOARD   **WHITE'S HOME BOARD**

LOGIC: This is another good blocking play, with an excellent chance afforded of White's making an additional blocking point on his next roll.

DOUBLE THREES

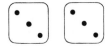

Assuming that Black opened, White moves two men from Black's one-point to Black's four-point, and two men from his own eight-point to his five-point.

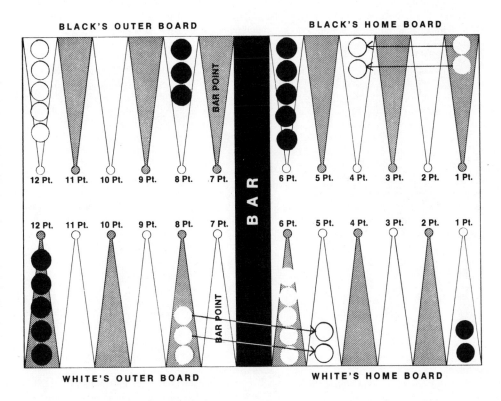

BLACK'S OUTER BOARD   BLACK'S HOME BOARD

12 Pt. 11 Pt. 10 Pt. 9 Pt. 8 Pt. 7 Pt.   BAR   6 Pt. 5 Pt. 4 Pt. 3 Pt. 2 Pt. 1 Pt.

12 Pt. 11 Pt. 10 Pt. 9 Pt. 8 Pt. 7 Pt.   BAR   6 Pt. 5 Pt. 4 Pt. 3 Pt. 2 Pt. 1 Pt.

WHITE'S OUTER BOARD   WHITE'S HOME BOARD

LOGIC: This move accomplishes running and blocking and also covers the key point (five-point) on White's home board.

DOUBLE FOURS

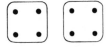

Assuming that Black opened, White moves two men from Black's one-point to Black's five-point, and two men from Black's twelve-point to his own nine-point.

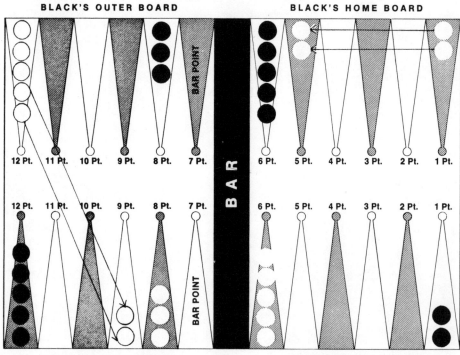

BLACK'S OUTER BOARD   **BLACK'S HOME BOARD**

WHITE'S OUTER BOARD   **WHITE'S HOME BOARD**

LOGIC: This move covers the opponent's home board's most important point and adds two men as builders to block the opponent.

DOUBLE FIVES

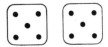

Assuming that Black opened, White moves two men from Black's twelve-point to his own three-point.

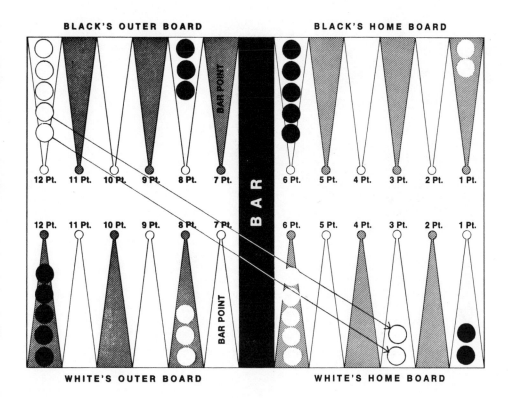

LOGIC: This is a bad roll. Unfortunately, this is the only safe way to play double fives.

DOUBLE SIXES

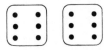

Assuming that Black opened, White moves two men from Black's one-point to Black's bar point, and two men from Black's twelve-point to his own bar point.

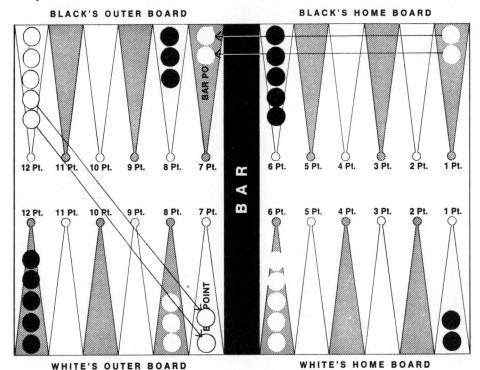

BLACK'S OUTER BOARD   **BLACK'S HOME BOARD**

12 Pt.   11 Pt.   10 Pt.   9 Pt.   8 Pt.   7 Pt.   **BAR**   6 Pt.   5 Pt.   4 Pt.   3 Pt.   2 Pt.   1 Pt.

WHITE'S OUTER BOARD   **WHITE'S HOME BOARD**

LOGIC: This roll is considered the best opening roll. It is the most advantageous in backgammon. Your chances of winning are greatly increased because you have a three-point prime and have covered your opponent's bar point. Double sixes also give a player a tremendous advantage in a running game.

LUCK VERSUS SKILL, AND THE ODDS

At this point, the beginner should become aware that backgammon is a game of luck and skill. No modern computer can figure the percentage of luck against skill in most gambling games. It is no different in backgammon. There is no question that a beginner will clip the ears off the pro if he rolls the proper dice.

It is also true that at a crucial point of a backgammon game, one perfect roll can change the entire game. This adds to the excitement and unpredictability of the game.

One can safely say that if two players of equal skill are engaged in a game, the one with the best dice will win. Likewise, of two players with equal luck, the one with the most skill will win.

Since luck does play such an important part in the game, the beginner should become aware of the odds. "Odds" is defined as being the ratio of probability that something is so, will occur, or is more likely to occur than something else.

In other words, in the course of a game you might find that double sixes are just what you need in order to execute your strategy. Keep in mind that the odds against rolling double sixes are thirty-five to one, definitely not much to bank on.

As far as odds are concerned, remember that rules are often made to be broken. The odds will serve you well at times; however, at other times, when you have learned how your opponent plays, they may well be dispensed with. This is true in backgammon as it is in bridge. Often conventional methods of play are changed upon confronting a special situation.

The list of odds below should be kept in the back of your mind. But do not use them with any other dice game; they will not work.

Here are the odds against rolling desired numbers or combinations of numbers on dice.

Number of Spaces Away	Approximate Odds Against
1	2 to 1 plus
2	2 to 1
3	3 to 2
4	7 to 5
5	7 to 5
6	Even plus
7	5 to 1
8	5 to 1
9	6 to 1
10	11 to 1
11	17 to 1

Backgammon

Number of Spaces Away	*Approximate Odds Against*
12	11 to 1
15	35 to 1
16	35 to 1
18	35 to 1
20	35 to 1
24	35 to 1

Here are the odds for rolling the proper combinations for bringing your man off the bar and back into the game.

Number of Points Covered (Blocked) On Opponent's Home Board	*Approximate Odds*
1	35 to 1 for
2	8 to 1 for
3	3 to 1 for
4	5 to 4 against
5	1½ to 1 against

Finally, keep in mind that in all games of chance the "feel" of the dice must be considered. If you have ever shot crap, recall how often you have felt either your number or a seven coming up.

It stands to reason that improving your skill in backgammon will also improve your chance of winning. If you become serious at the game and play enough, your skill will come out ahead of your luck in the long run.

chapter four

A Beginner's Sample Game of Backgammon

This sample game is designed to demonstrate a basic game of backgammon. You will learn the general principles of running and blocking if you follow these instructions. First, set up your board properly, then move the men according to the instructions and carefully read and digest the comments.

Since in the game of backgammon two games are almost never alike, many different situations arise. The most important factor that a beginner must keep in mind when starting to play is: *Leave as few men exposed as possible.* The temptation of the average beginner is to move his men willy-nilly, leaving several men open. The moment you sit down to play the first game, try to plan your moves. In other words, *plan your work and work your plan.* It may be wrong, but this is better than not having any scheme in mind. If you must leave a man exposed, try to do it on your opponent's home board, where should you be hit, the distance back into the game is not as great as it would be if you were hit on your own home board.

Above all, take your chances early in the game, when your opponent's home board is open and you have plenty of opportunity to come in should you be knocked off.

THE SAMPLE GAME

The two players have rolled the dice to determine who starts the game. White's three has topped Black's one.

MOVE # ONE: White moves one man from his eight-point to his five-point, and one man from his six-point to his five-point.

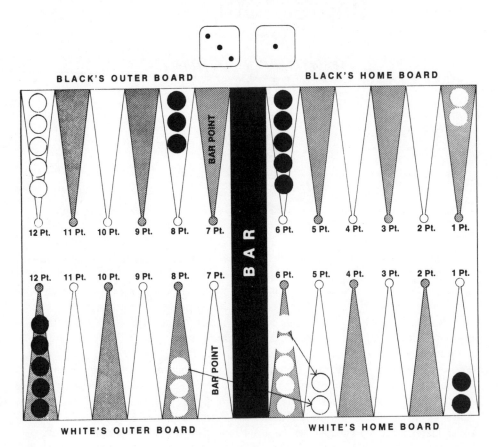

A Beginner's Sample Game of Backgammon

MOVE # TWO: Black moves one man from his eight-point to his four-point, and one man from his six-point to his four-point.

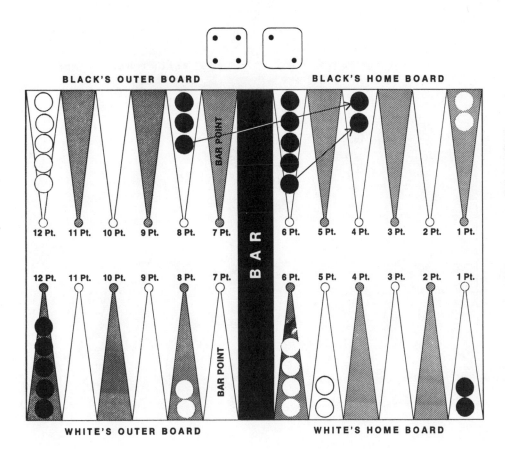

MOVE # THREE: White moves two men from Black's twelve-point to his own bar point.

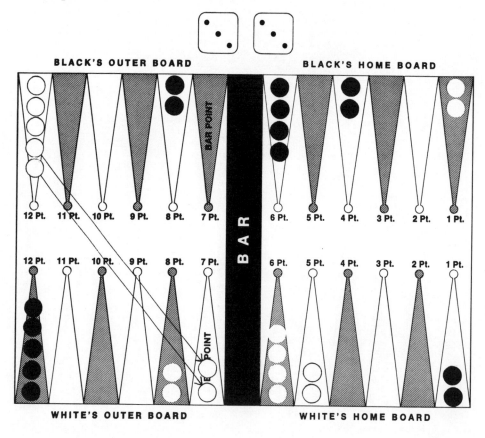

LOGIC: By making this move, White now has a four-point block from his five-point to his eight-point. He should now hope for a good roll to make a five-point block.

MOVE # FOUR: Black moves one man from White's twelve-point to his own eight-point, and one man from White's one-point to White's three-point.

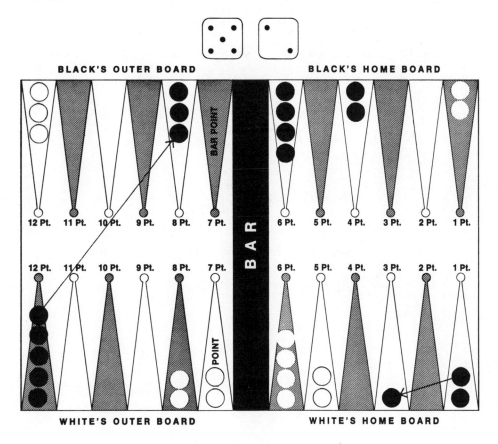

LOGIC: The reason for Black's moving a two in this manner is that he is finding it much more difficult now to run out of his opponent's home board. Should he cover the three-point on his opponent's board a lucky roll of double sixes will get him out. This is the only double throw which could get him out.

Backgammon

MOVE # FIVE: White moves two men from his six-point to his four-point.

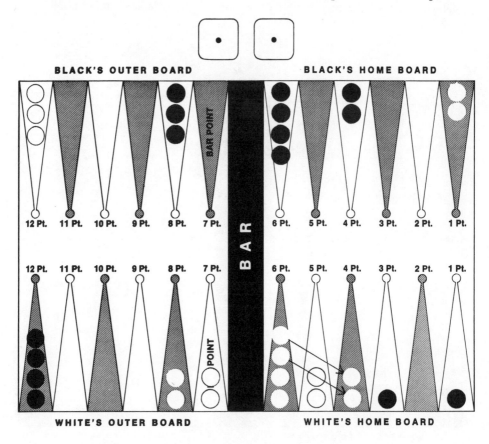

LOGIC: The double accomplishes a five-point block.

MOVE # SIX: Black moves one man from White's one-point to White's three-point, and one man from White's twelve-point to his own ten-point.

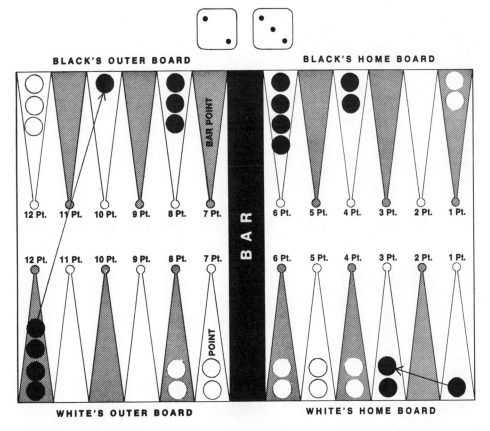

LOGIC: This covers his exposed man and brings up a builder in hopes of getting another point to block White's two men on Black's one-point.

MOVE # SEVEN: White moves one man from Black's one-point to Black's ten-point.

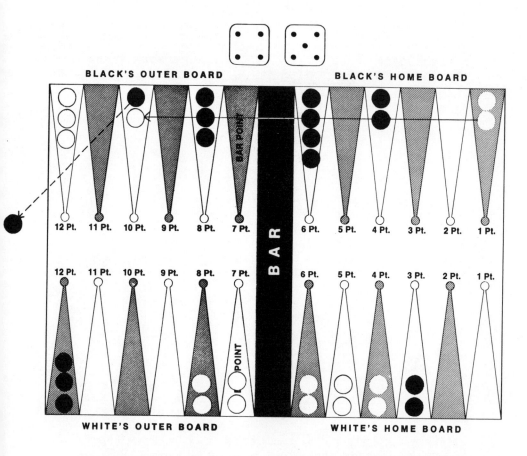

LOGIC: This is a very lucky roll. White takes Black's man "off," placing it on the bar. This man now has to "come in" (also called "come on") all the way back on White's home board and start going around again.

PAUSE: At this point both players should determine who's ahead. Both players should constantly keep this in mind in order to plan strategy. White is clearly ahead as Black has one man off plus two men on White's home board. White should now play a running game and Black should now think of staying "back" with the hope of catching an exposed White man *or* of thrusting ahead on a very lucky roll.

A Beginner's Sample Game of Backgammon

MOVE # EIGHT: Black's man on the bar comes into play on White's three-point. Black moves his other man from White's twelve-point to his own nine-point.

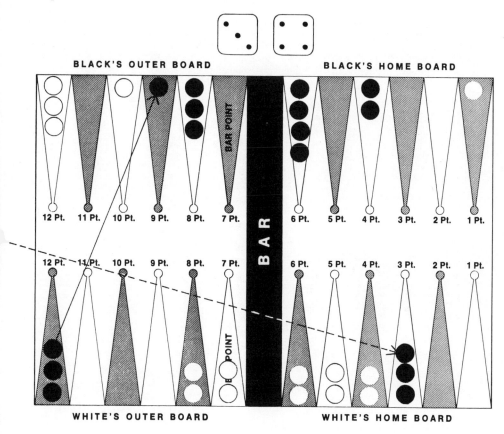

MOVE # NINE: White moves one man from Black's ten-point to his own nine-point, and one man from Black's twelve-point to his own nine-point.

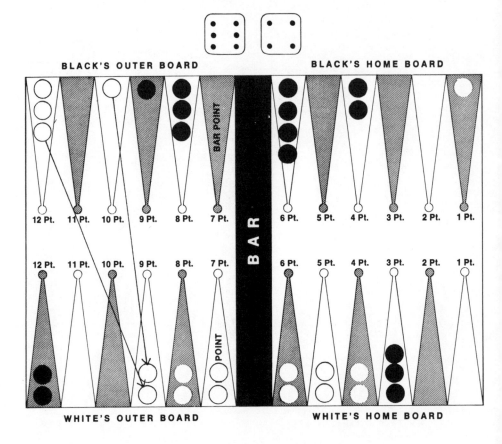

LOGIC: White has created a "prime." A prime is six consecutive blocked points. White's advantage is now tremendous, as there is no way that Black can get out from White's home board until White moves some of his men off his prime. This is known as "breaking a prime."

A Beginner's Sample Game of Backgammon

MOVE # TEN: Black moves one man from his nine-point to his five-point, and one man from his six-point to his five-point.

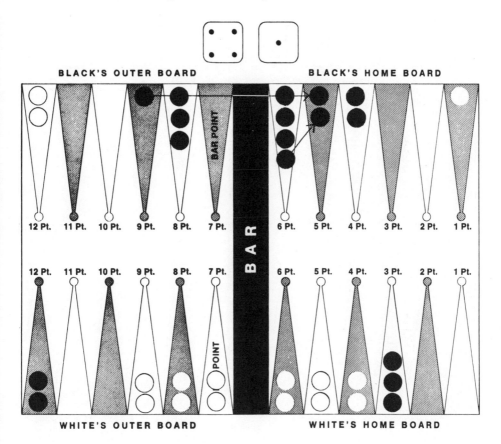

LOGIC: Although Black is considerably behind he still hopes to block White's man located on his own one-point. If he succeeds, White will eventually have to break his prime. The chances of this plan succeeding are small, as Black would have to roll very lucky dice.

MOVE # ELEVEN: White moves one man from Black's one-point to Black's nine-point.

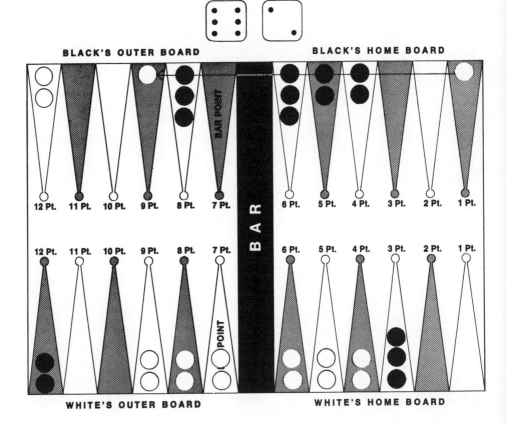

MOVE # TWELVE: Black moves one man from his eight-point to his five-point.

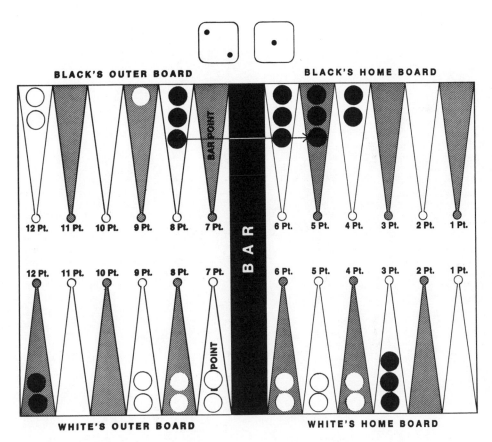

LOGIC: Black brings another builder onto his home board, so that in the event he should send one of White's men home, White would have difficulty in getting out of Black's home board. Black must also hope to make his next block on his three-point, thus establishing four consecutive blocking points.

MOVE # THIRTEEN: White moves one man from Black's nine-point to his own five-point.

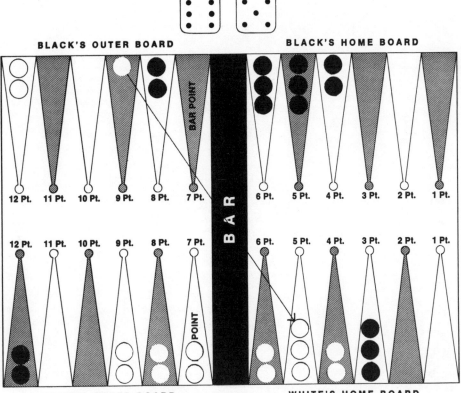

MOVE # FOURTEEN: Black moves one man from his eight-point to his three-point, and one man from his five-point to his three-point.

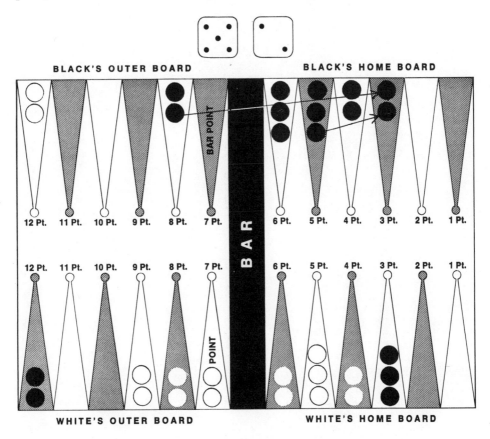

LOGIC: Although Black's chances of winning are still small, he is accomplishing what he is trying to do as described in move # twelve.

MOVE # FIFTEEN: White moves one man from Black's twelve-point to his own eight-point, and one man from Black's twelve-point to his own nine-point.

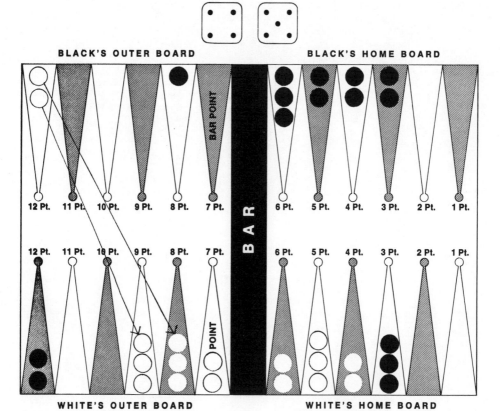

A Beginner's Sample Game of Backgammon

MOVE # SIXTEEN: Black moves one man from White's twelve-point to his own two-point.

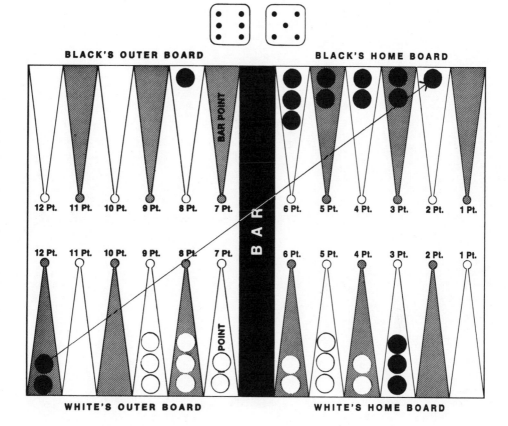

MOVE # SEVENTEEN: White moves one man from his nine-point to his six-point, and one man from his eight-point to his two-point.

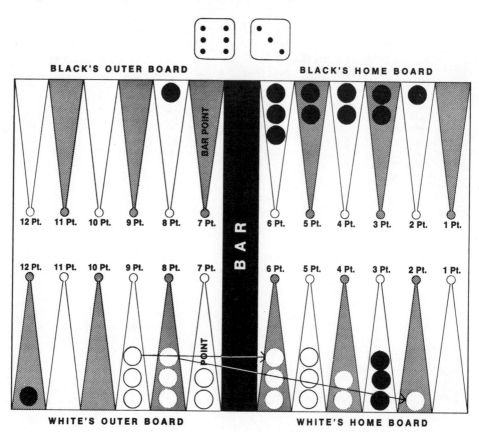

A Beginner's Sample Game of Backgammon

MOVE # EIGHTEEN: Black moves one man from his eight-point to his two-point, and one man from White's twelve-point to his own eleven-point.

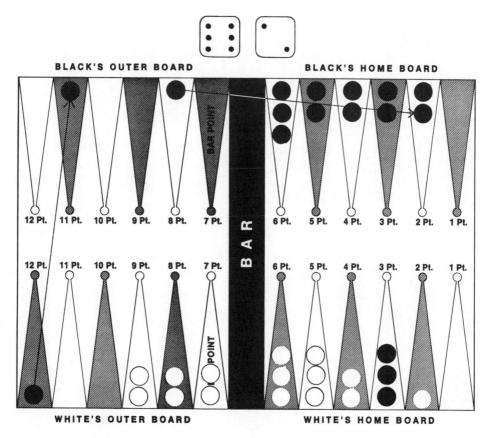

LOGIC: Black now has a five-point prime on his home board.

MOVE # NINETEEN: White moves two men from his nine-point to his five-point, and two men from his eight-point to his four-point.

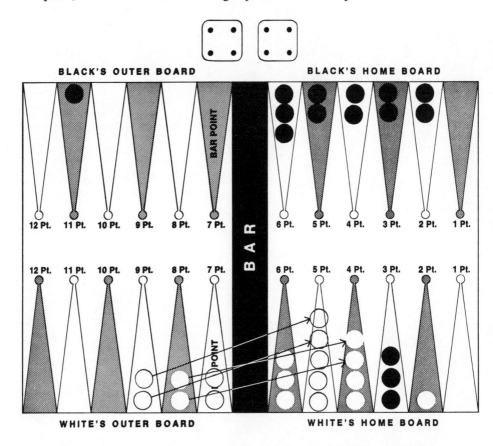

LOGIC: White is bringing his men into his home board as fast as possible in order to bear these men off and continue his advantage. Black should try to keep two men on White's board, hoping that in bearing off, White may leave a man exposed. This would give Black a chance to hit him and make him start in from Black's home board again.

A Beginner's Sample Game of Backgammon

MOVE # TWENTY: Black moves one man from White's three-point to White's eleven-point.

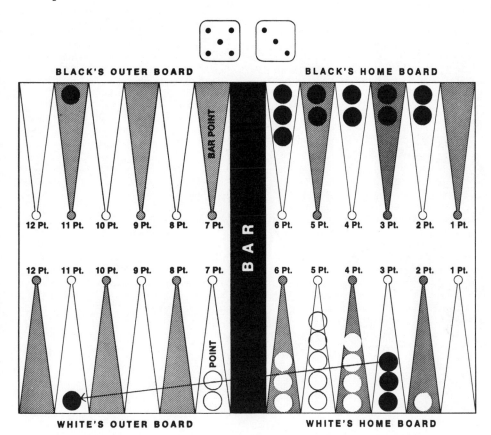

MOVE # TWENTY-ONE: White moves one man from his bar point to his four-point, and one man from his bar point to his one-point.

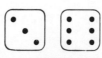

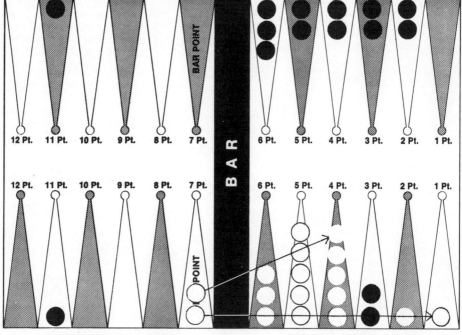

MOVE # TWENTY-TWO: Black moves one man from his eleven-point to his bar point, and one man from White's eleven-point to White's twelve-point.

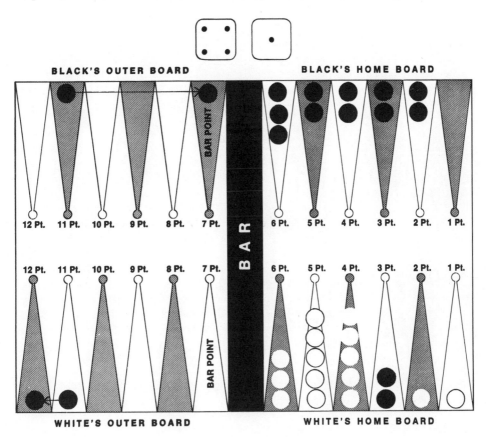

BLACK'S OUTER BOARD **BLACK'S HOME BOARD**

BAR POINT

12 Pt. 11 Pt. 10 Pt. 9 Pt. 8 Pt. 7 Pt. | B A R | 6 Pt. 5 Pt. 4 Pt. 3 Pt. 2 Pt. 1 Pt.

12 Pt. 11 Pt. 10 Pt. 9 Pt. 8 Pt. 7 Pt. | 6 Pt. 5 Pt. 4 Pt. 3 Pt. 2 Pt. 1 Pt.

BAR POINT

WHITE'S OUTER BOARD **WHITE'S HOME BOARD**

LOGIC: This move was made in hope of throwing a six on the next roll so that Black could then establish a six-man prime, in the event that he is lucky enough to send one of White's men to his home board later.

85

MOVE # TWENTY-THREE: White moves one man from his six-point and bears off. He also moves one man from his two-point and bears off.

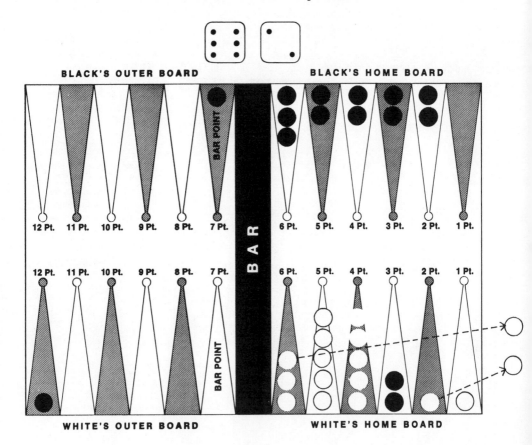

LOGIC: Since all of White's men are now on his home board, he can start bearing them off. He begins with the highest point (the six-point). He can then bear off accordingly, placing these men outside the backgammon board.

MOVE # TWENTY-FOUR: Black moves one man from White's twelve-point to his own ten-point.

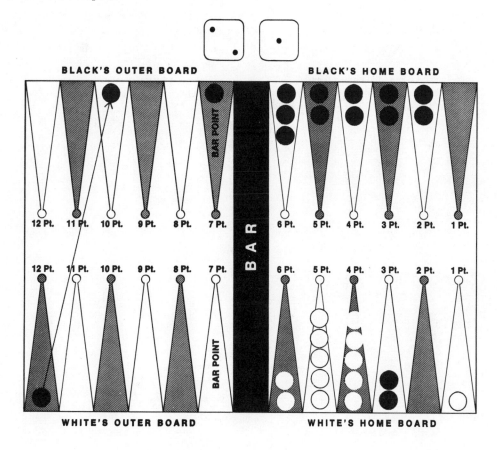

LOGIC: The strategy here is the same as for Black's play in move # twenty-two.

Backgammon

MOVE # TWENTY-FIVE: White moves one man from his six-point and bears off. The other man he moves from his four-point to his one-point.

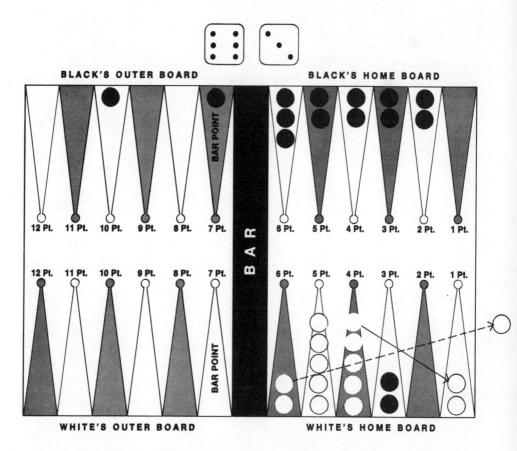

BLACK'S OUTER BOARD   BLACK'S HOME BOARD

WHITE'S OUTER BOARD   WHITE'S HOME BOARD

LOGIC: This is an extremely unlucky roll, as White *must* play his six-point off. He cannot "safe" his now exposed man remaining on the six-point because of Black's point blocking. The reasoning behind covering his one-point is in anticipation that should Black later send him home, he can in turn send Black home. White will have three points covered.

A Beginner's Sample Game of Backgammon

MOVE # TWENTY-SIX: Black moves one man from White's three-point to White's six-point, and then the same man from White's six-point to White's eleven-point.

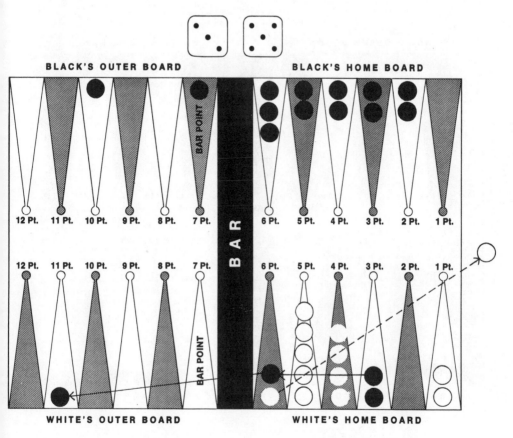

LOGIC: Black has knocked off the exposed man on White's six-point and continued on his way. First he plays his three and then his five.

MOVE # TWENTY-SEVEN: White cannot come in.

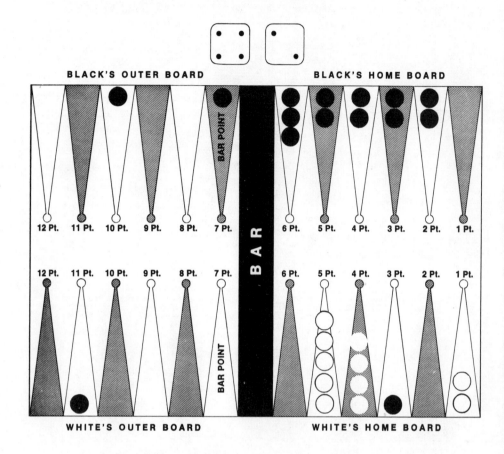

LOGIC: White cannot bring his man in on Black's two-point or Black's four-point, proving that Black's desperate strategy has paid off. White forfeits his move until he can bring his man back into the game with the right roll (this would be a one).

MOVE # TWENTY-EIGHT: Black moves one man from White's eleven-point to his own nine-point.

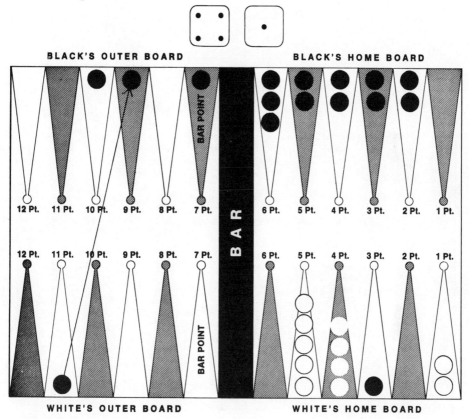

LOGIC: Black still hopes to make his bar point, which would give him a six-man prime.

Backgammon

MOVE # TWENTY-NINE: White brings one man in on Black's one-point, and further moves his man from Black's one-point to Black's bar point.

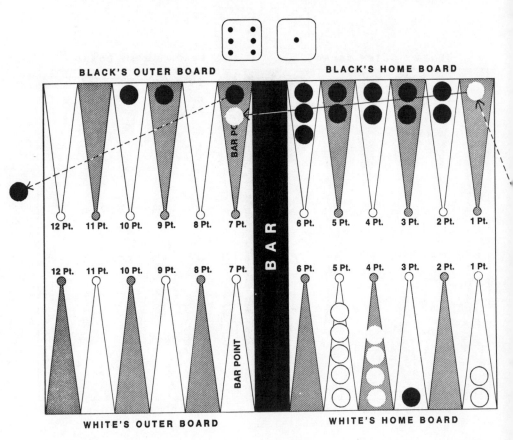

LOGIC: White knocks off one of Black's men. So far, this is the luckiest roll of the game. (See Chapter Three on odds.)

MOVE # THIRTY: Black brings one man in on White's six-point, and moves one man from his own ten-point to his six-point.

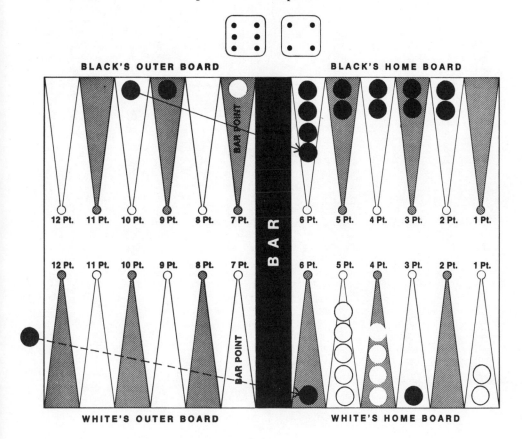

Backgammon

MOVE # THIRTY-ONE: White moves one man from Black's bar point to Black's eleven-point.

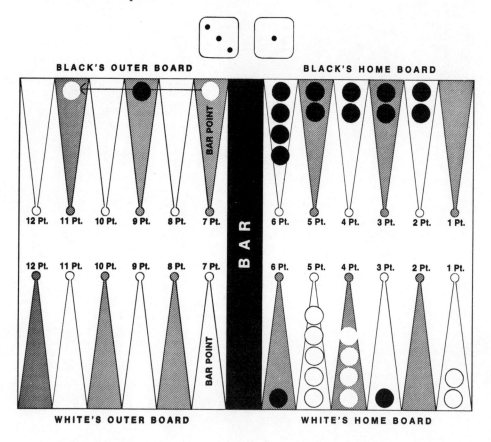

LOGIC: In so doing White has not given Black a direct shot and is trying to run home as fast as possible.

A Beginner's Sample Game of Backgammon

MOVE # THIRTY-TWO: Black moves one man from his nine-point to his four-point, and one man from his six-point to his two-point.

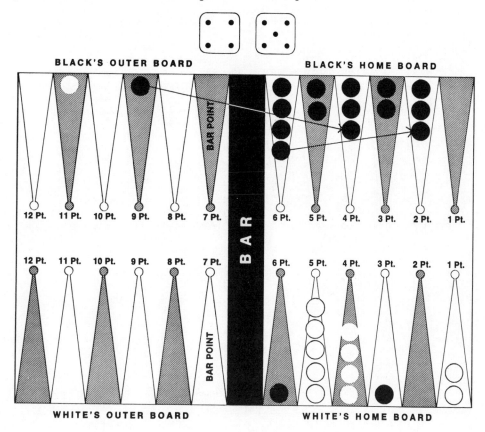

LOGIC: Black's last chance to knock White's only exposed man off is with the two men he has on White's home board. He now hopes that White may roll a number such as a five or six with a one or two so that he would have two chances of knocking White off.

Backgammon

MOVE # THIRTY-THREE: White moves one man from Black's eleven-point to his own four-point.

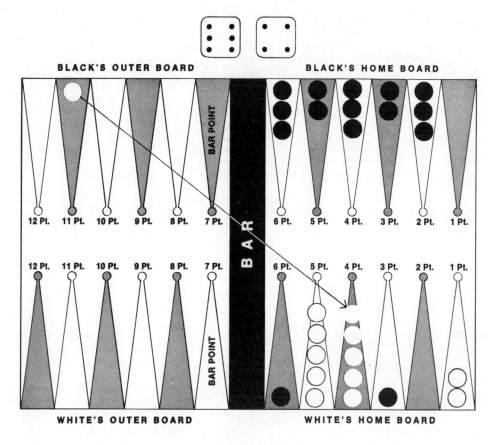

BLACK'S OUTER BOARD   BLACK'S HOME BOARD

WHITE'S OUTER BOARD   WHITE'S HOME BOARD

LOGIC: This was a lucky roll and White has all of his men home again.

A Beginner's Sample Game of Backgammon

MOVE # THIRTY-FOUR: Black moves one man from White's six-point to White's twelve-point.

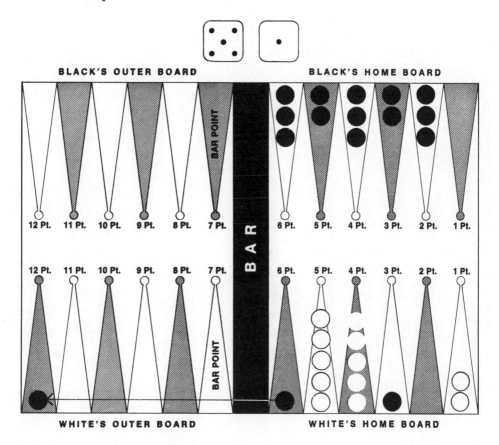

Backgammon

MOVE # THIRTY-FIVE: White moves four men from his five-point and bears off.

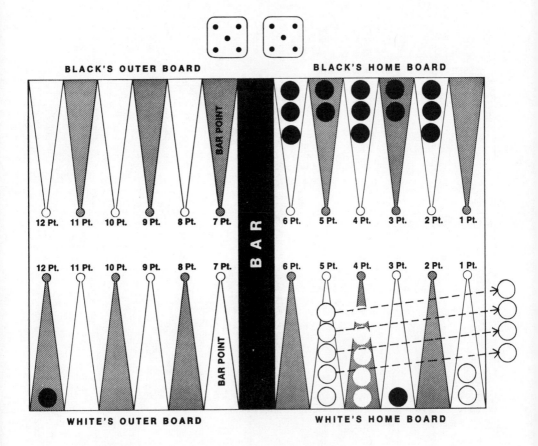

LOGIC: One man is left exposed. White should be a little nervous now, for if Black rolls a two on the next round, he will knock him off again.

MOVE # THIRTY-SIX: Black moves one man from his four-point to his one-point, and one man from White's twelve-point to his own nine-point.

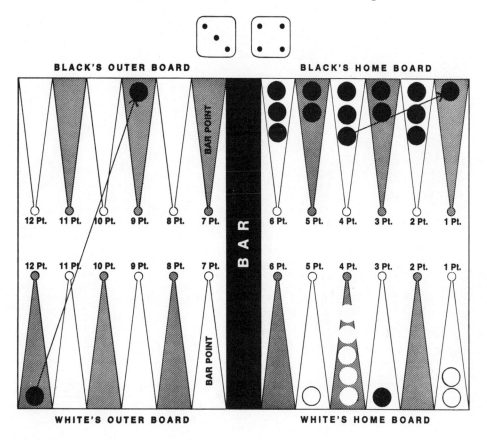

LOGIC: Black keeps one man back on White's home board with a slight hope that White may leave another man exposed. This is his last chance.

MOVE # THIRTY-SEVEN: White moves one man from his five-point and bears him off, and another man from his four-point and bears him off.

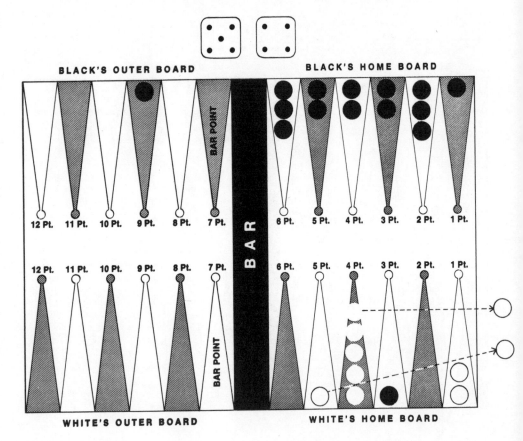

MOVE # THIRTY-EIGHT: Black moves one man from his nine-point to his three-point.

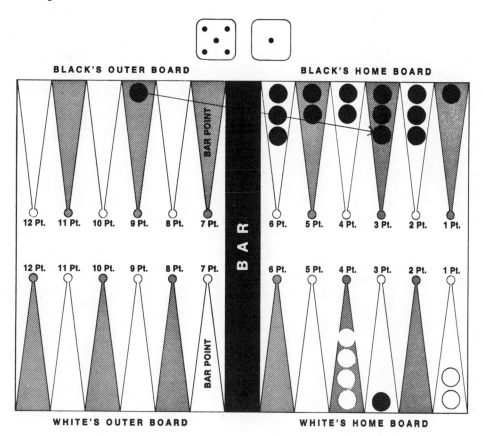

101

MOVE # THIRTY-NINE: White moves one man from his four-point and bears him off, and one man from his four-point to his two-point.

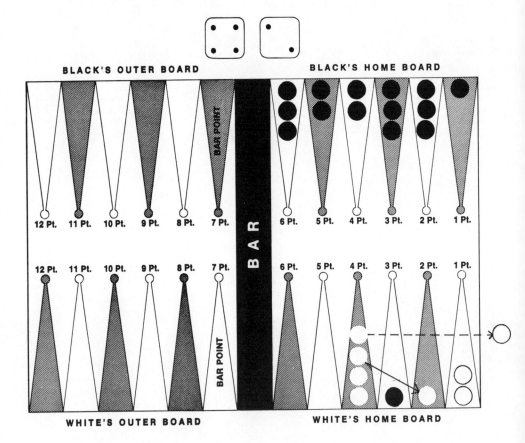

A Beginner's Sample Game of Backgammon

MOVE # FORTY: Black moves one man from White's three-point to his own eleven-point.

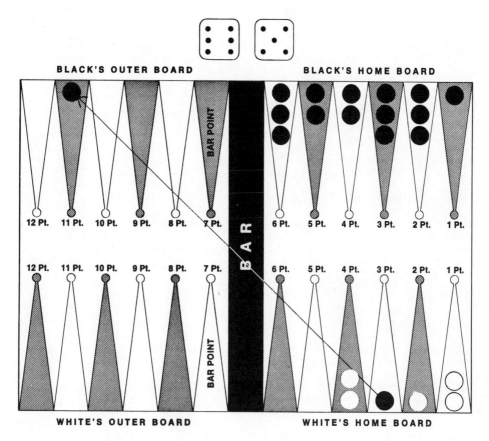

LOGIC: No hope—Black runs like mad to avoid a gammon.

Backgammon

MOVE # FORTY-ONE: White moves one man from his four-point and bears off, and one man from his four-point to his one-point.

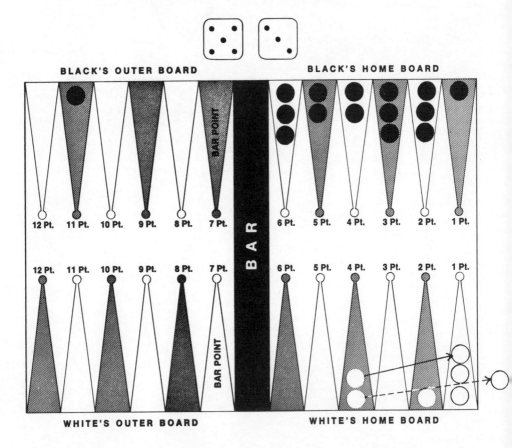

LOGIC: If a six or five should be rolled and there are no men on these points, then bear off from the next lowest number.

MOVE # FORTY-TWO: Black moves one man from his eleven-point to his five-point, and bears off two men from his three-point.

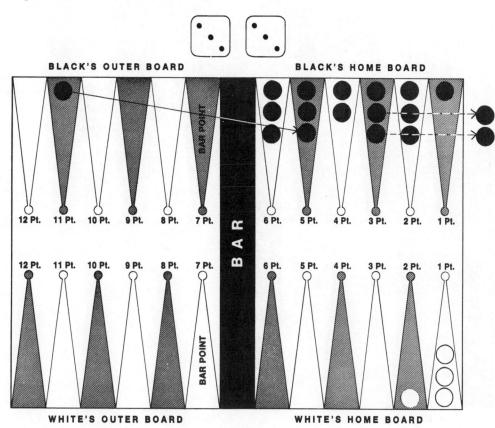

105

MOVE # FORTY-THREE: White moves one man from his two-point and bears off, and one man from his one-point and bears off.

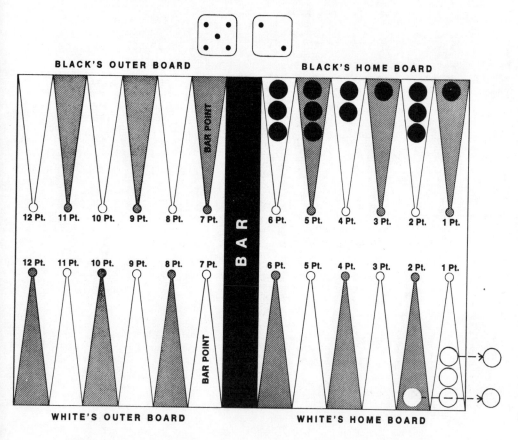

It is obvious that White has won the game.

chapter five

The Running Game

Of the two basic strategies involved in the game of backgammon, the running game is the offensive. If good dice rolls have enabled you to get your two back men off of your opponent's one-point early in the game (for example, an opening roll of 6/5 followed by a 6/2, 6/3, or 6/4), you should immediately play a running game. This, of course, is true only if you have not been hit on the way.

In the game illustrated below both players have moved their back men out early in the game; therefore both should play a running game. This situation

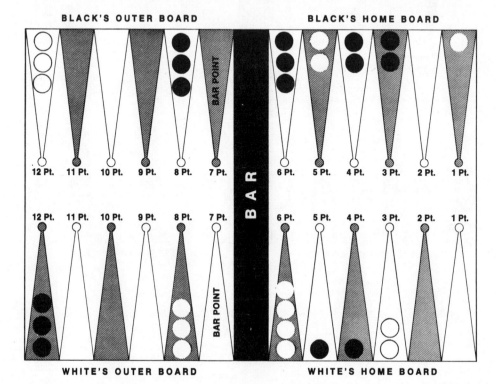

BLACK'S OUTER BOARD   BLACK'S HOME BOARD

12 Pt.   11 Pt.   10 Pt.   9 Pt.   8 Pt.   7 Pt.   BAR   6 Pt.   5 Pt.   4 Pt.   3 Pt.   2 Pt.   1 Pt.

12 Pt.   11 Pt.   10 Pt.   9 Pt.   8 Pt.   7 Pt.   BAR   6 Pt.   5 Pt.   4 Pt.   3 Pt.   2 Pt.   1 Pt.

WHITE'S OUTER BOARD   WHITE'S HOME BOARD

(of both players having moved their back men out early in the game) does not occur frequently, as almost always an advantage is established along the way and tactics must be changed.

Black is playing a running game and at present has a slight advantage over White. Black only has two men on White's home board, whereas White has three on Black's home board. Black's strategy should be to run like hell. He should run even if it means leaving a man exposed on his outer board. It is Black's roll.

MOVE # ONE: Black moves one man from White's four-point to White's twelve-point.

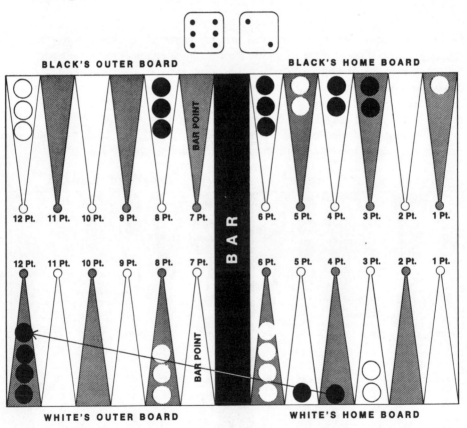

LOGIC: Black is running and covering an exposed man.

MOVE # TWO: White moves one man from his eight-point to his four-point, and one man from his six-point to his three-point.

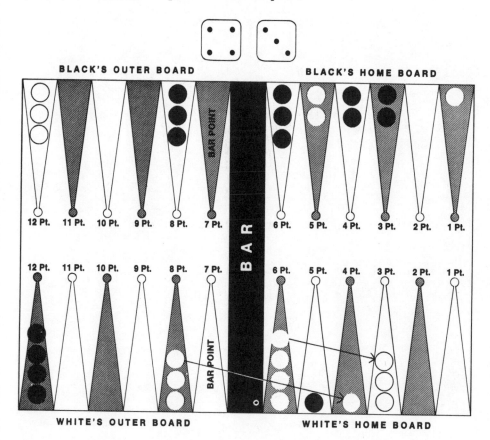

BLACK'S OUTER BOARD

BLACK'S HOME BOARD

WHITE'S OUTER BOARD

WHITE'S HOME BOARD

LOGIC: White could have moved the four from Black's one-point to Black's five-point, where he already has two men. But White is *not in a position to run*. If the dice run even for the rest of the game, Black should win. So White's only chance is by staying back with three men in two different positions on Black's home board. At the same time, he is now also working on getting an additional point on his own home board.

MOVE # THREE: Black moves one man from White's five-point to White's ten-point.

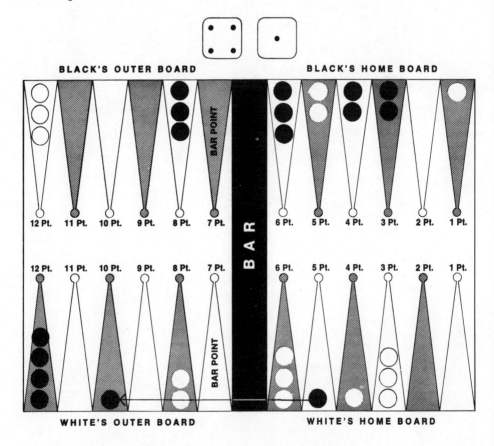

LOGIC: Black's strategy is to run. Even though he leaves a man exposed where White can hit him (with a three or a ten), the chance is worth it. Should he be hit, he can come back into play on four different points on White's home board.

MOVE # FOUR: White moves one man from Black's twelve-point to his own bar point, and one man from his own six-point to his four-point.

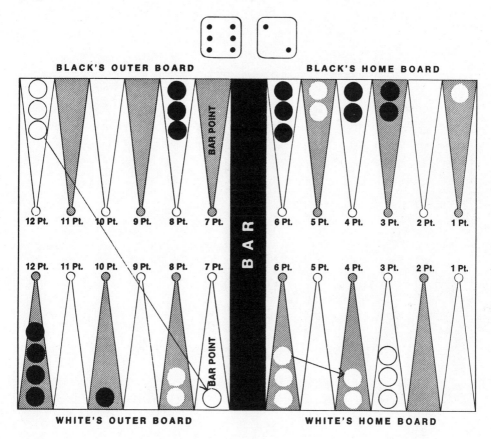

LOGIC: White establishes another point on his home board. This is important because, should he ever hit Black, Black now has only three points left to come back in on.

MOVE # FIVE: Black moves one man from White's ten-point to his own nine-point, and one man from White's twelve-point to his own nine-point.

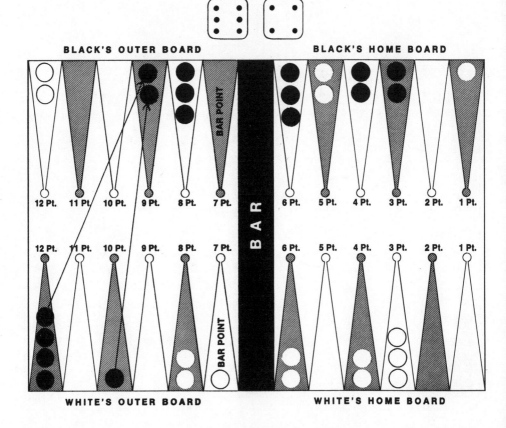

LOGIC: Black continues his running game by establishing another point close to home on his nine-point.

MOVE # SIX: White moves one man from his eight-point to his two-point, and one man from his three-point to his two-point.

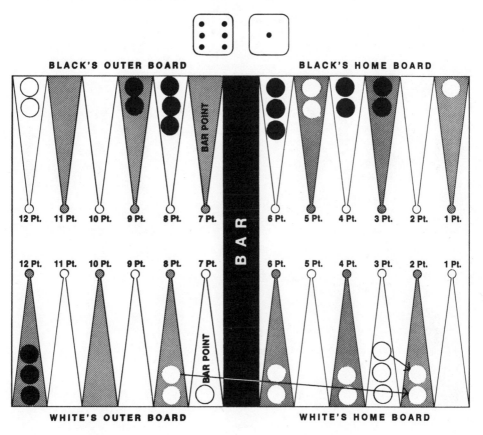

LOGIC: White has established four points on his home board.

MOVE # SEVEN: Black moves one man from White's twelve-point to his own bar point, and one man from his own eight-point to his bar point.

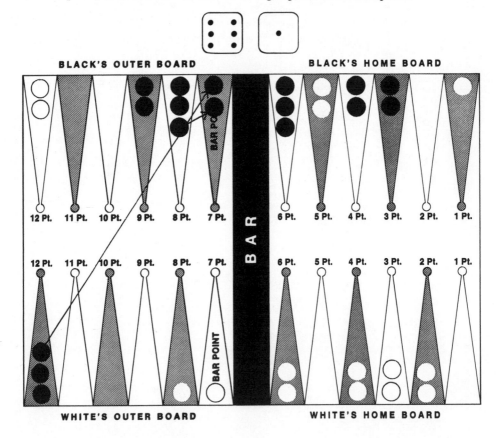

LOGIC: Black's running game is continuing successfully. He now has six points covered on his home board and outer board, with one void where White has two men on Black's five-point. Unless he has very bad dice, Black should be home in a breeze.

chapter six

The Blocking Game

You always play a blocking game when your opponent has thrown better dice than you and is obviously playing a running game. It is a defensive strategy.

Your obvious defense, unless you have a series of lucky rolls on the dice, is to try to block your opponent from getting out of your home board.

The game has progressed to the point in the illustration.

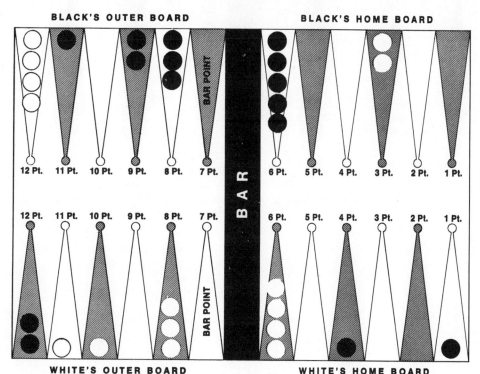

First of all, there is no question but that Black is ahead.

MOVE # ONE: White moves one man from Black's twelve-point to his own nine-point, and one man from his own ten-point to his nine-point.

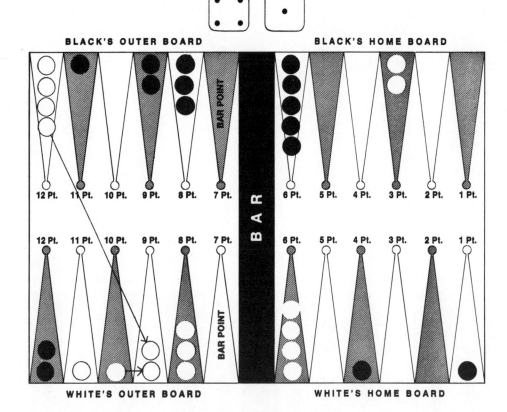

LOGIC: White is working toward a "side prime." A side prime is any prime outside of his own home board. He now has three points going for him on the side prime, one on his nine-point, one on his eight-point, and one on his six-point.

MOVE # TWO: Black moves one man from White's one-point to White's four-point, and one man from his own eleven-point to his nine-point.

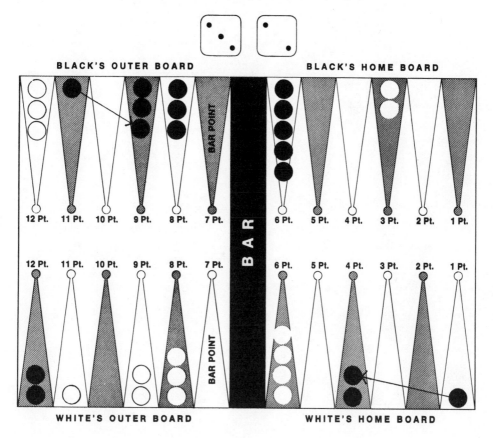

LOGIC: Black now has one important point on White's home board and is also beginning to block White from getting out of Black's home board.

MOVE # THREE: White moves three men from Black's twelve-point to his own ten-point, and one man from his own six-point to his three-point.

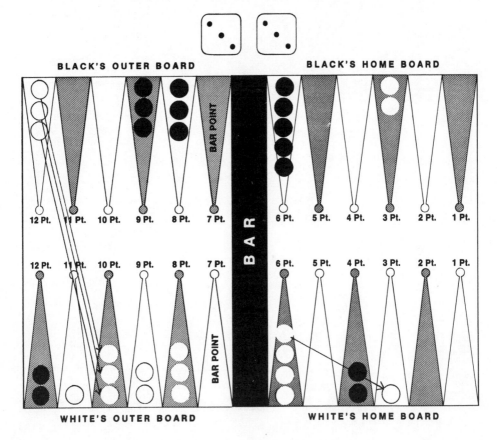

LOGIC: The reason White didn't make his fourth three move safe by playing it from his eleven-point to his eight-point is because he is trying at all costs to construct a side prime. So then, he now has an additional builder to the exposed builder on White's eleven-point.

MOVE # FOUR: Black moves one man from his eight-point to his four-point, and one man from his six-point to his four-point.

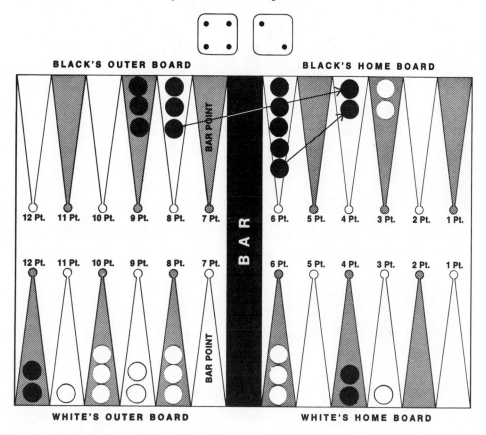

LOGIC: Up to now, Black's only weakness was that he had only one point covered on his home board. This move gives him an additional point on his home board as well as an extra block.

Backgammon

MOVE # FIVE: White moves one man from his ten-point to his bar point, and one man from his eight-point to his bar point.

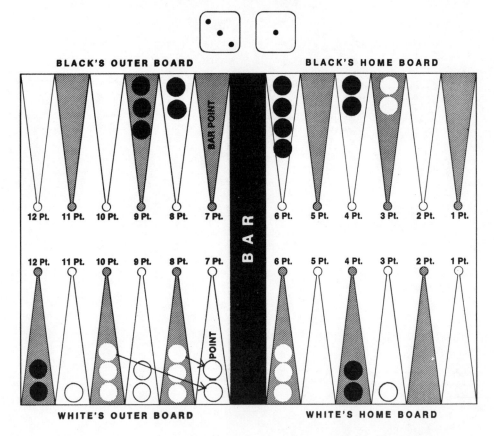

LOGIC: White now has a five-man prime (five covered points in a row). The only way Black can move a man out of White's home board is by rolling a one and six.

MOVE # SIX: Black moves two men from White's twelve-point to his own one-point.

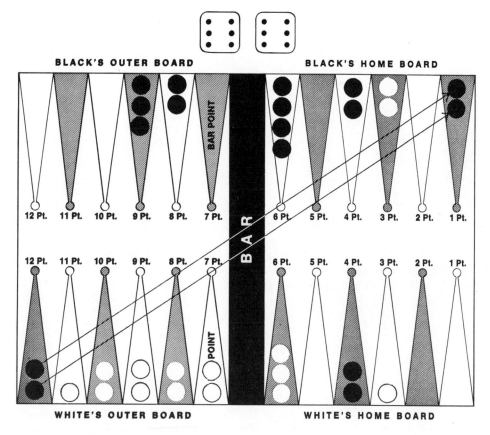

LOGIC: Ordinarily double sixes is a very good roll in a running game. In this case it isn't. The reason Black continued on to his one-point instead of playing his second two sixes from his eight point to his two-point is that he is getting desperate. White's blocking game is working. However, by playing it this way, Black has White's possible double fives and double sixes blocked, which is better than having White's double fours and double sixes blocked.

Unless Black throws very lucky dice, White should win the game. If Black throws high dice, he will have to move his men from his eight-point or his nine-point. This would give White an additional opportunity to get out of Black's home board.

chapter seven

The Back Game

By reason of luck, one player finds himself at a disadvantage in having four or more men on his opponent's home board. (See diagram.) He now must play what is known as a back game.

It has been proven that chances of winning a back game are not the best. Some quote the odds of winning as three to one against. This type of game should not be attempted unless you are absolutely forced into it and really have no other choice.

There is a backgammon player in the Southwest who always plays back games and needless to say continuously loses games and money. Why he continues in this masochistic machination remains a mystery.

There is another player, one of the finest in the entire world, who learned backgammon by playing back games most of the time. It occurred in this manner. The gentleman happened to be a great bridge and gin player and he knew that, without exceptional luck, chances of winning are small when playing with an expert. Therefore, he devised a strategy designed to upset his opponent's style and type of game. He decided that rather than play a running game to start, he would try to pick off his opponent's men wherever and whenever possible, and leave many of his own men open all over the board. Although at first he lost most of the time, he developed a style of his own. His strategy included figuring out how many men should be back and in what position they should be, as well as ascertaining the position of his opponent's men and points. He is unquestionably the greatest back game player in the world today.

A back game is the type of game played when a player finds himself so far behind that he must concentrate on getting more men back on his opponent's home board (usually four or five). Further, he must forget his running game. In most cases, if he has only three men back, he should not pursue the idea of a back game. If his opponent doubles when he has three men back, he should not take the double. The odds of losing a back game are three to one. These odds are diminished a bit if the back game player controls the doubling block.

The play for the sample back game has progressed to this point:

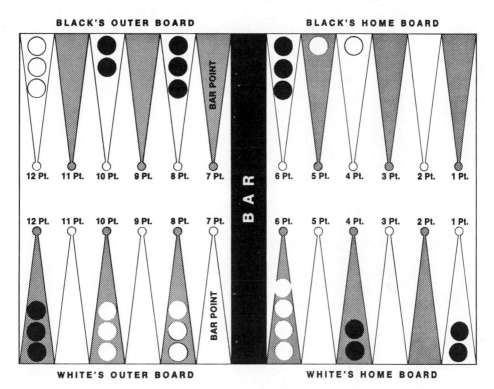

Black cannot think of playing a running game. His only chance now is to lay and wait while White brings all his men home. He can then start hitting White's men as they become exposed on their way home. In order to do this, Black must have at least four men back and in some cases may even try to get a fifth man back in order to keep his back game going. His future plan as White gets out of Black's home board is to start a prime on his own home board. If possible, he should now gradually build his prime from his six-point down.

MOVE # ONE: White moves one man from Black's four-point to Black's twelve-point.

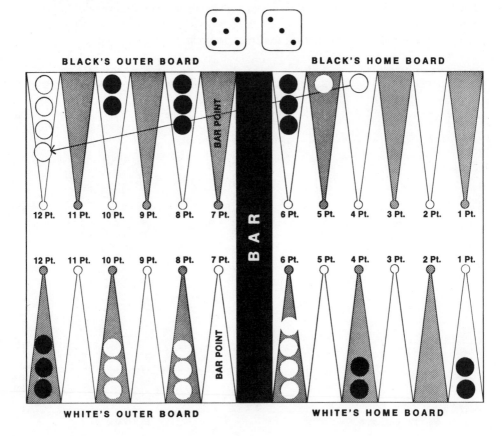

LOGIC: White makes one man safe and brings an additional builder in for his side prime.

MOVE # TWO: Black moves one man from his six-point to his four-point, and one man from his eight-point to his four-point.

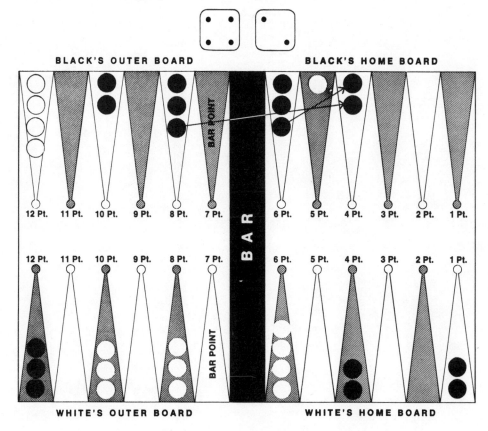

LOGIC: Although Black wishes he could make his five-point, this might be termed a second choice. It will help him plan for a prime on his home board.

MOVE # THREE: White moves one man from his ten-point to his bar point, and one man from his eight-point to his bar point.

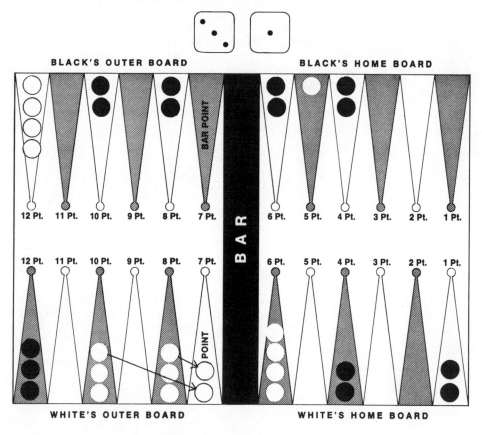

LOGIC: White now has five points fairly close together and needs double fours or twos for a side prime.

MOVE # FOUR: Black moves one man from White's twelve-point to his own ten-point.

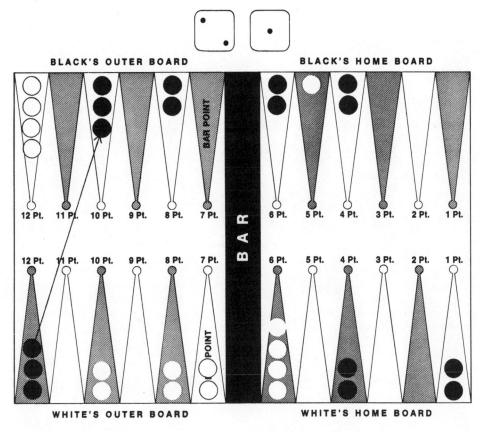

LOGIC: This is not a good roll. All it accomplishes is playing a man safe.

Backgammon

MOVE # FIVE: White moves one man from Black's five-point to his own eight-point. He then moves two men from Black's twelve-point to his own bar point.

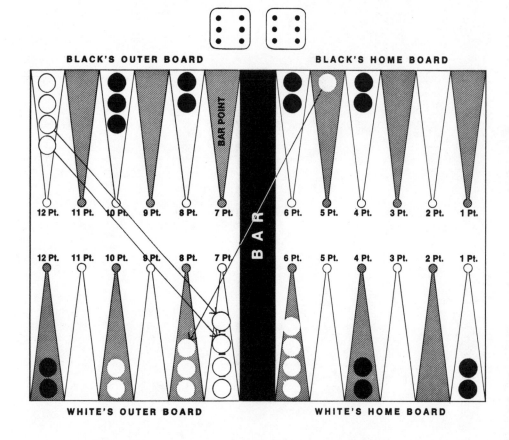

LOGIC: Although White has not been able to make his side prime, he has avoided being hit by Black should he roll a one, five, or three.

MOVE # SIX: Black moves one man from his ten-point to his five-point, and one man from his eight-point to his five-point.

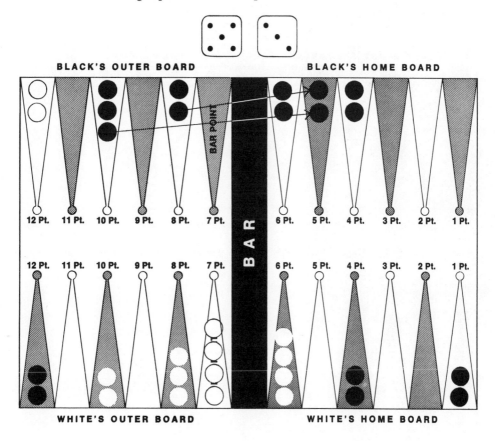

LOGIC: Black is starting to build a prime from his six-point down.

MOVE # SEVEN: White moves one man from Black's twelve-point to his own six-point.

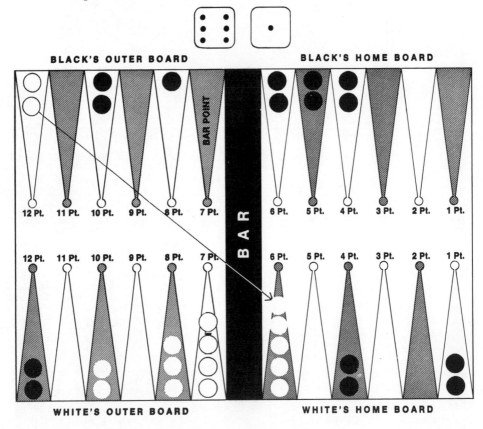

LOGIC: This is not a good roll. It is strictly speaking a safe play, bringing one more man into the home board.

MOVE # EIGHT: Black moves two men from White's twelve-point to his own three-point.

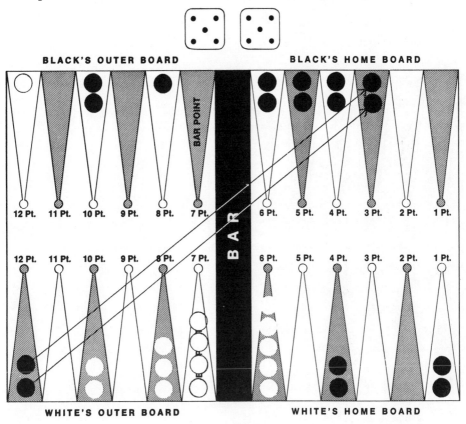

LOGIC: Black has now created a four-man prime.

MOVE # NINE: White moves one man from his six-point to his five-point, and one man from his eight-point to his five-point.

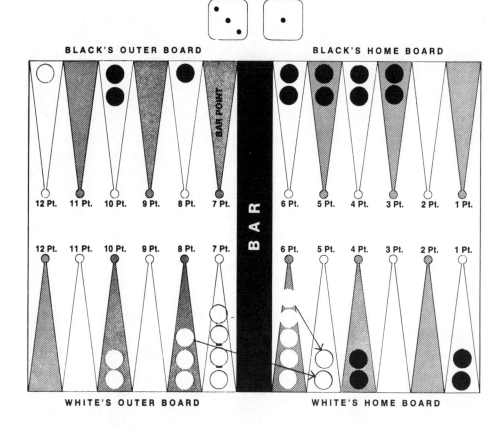

LOGIC: This gives White a four-point prime. The only way White can get hit is by Black rolling 5/4.

MOVE # TEN: Black moves one man from his ten-point to his two-point.

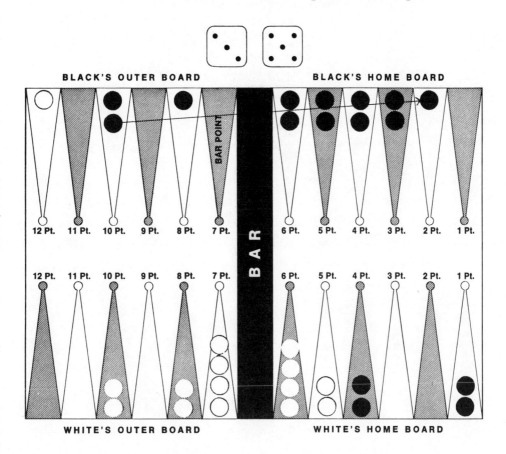

LOGIC: Black continues to build his prime as planned and now needs only a six or eight on his next roll to accomplish this.

Backgammon

MOVE # ELEVEN: White moves one man from his eight-point to his two-point, and one man from his bar point to his two-point.

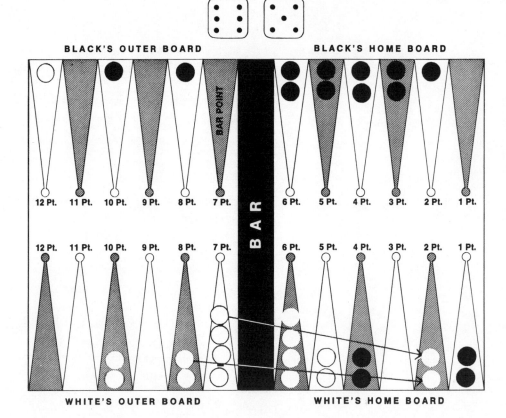

LOGIC: This is a bad roll in that White has to leave a man exposed on his eight-point.

134

MOVE # TWELVE: Black moves one man from his eight-point to his two-point, and one man from White's four-point to White's eight-point.

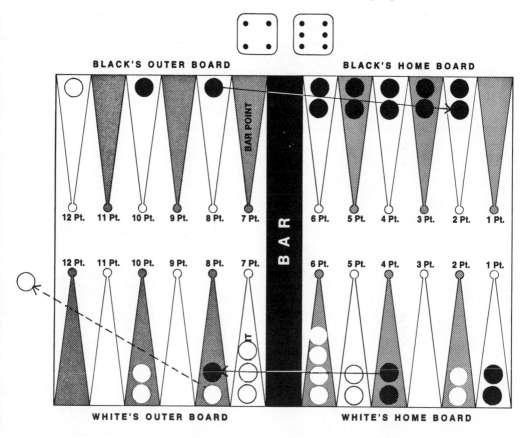

LOGIC: This is a lucky roll. Black has hit White's exposed man on White's eight-point. The only way White can come back is by rolling a one and six. Even then, he could be hit again. Black should win the game.

There are many examples of back games where the man who plays the back game has two points covered on his opponent's home board in places other than those illustrated above. Generally speaking, in playing a back game, it is preferable to have the one-point and the four-point or lower blocked, rather than to have the five-point and the one-point blocked. The gap from the five-point to the one-point is not considered to be as advantageous as that from the four-point down.

And further, if there is a chance of creating the beginning of a back game by making two points adjacently (one and two, two and three, three and four) you should do it. This will make it more difficult for your opponent to come home without exposing himself.

Backgammon

The back game illustrated is only one of the many possible. You might face a situation where your opponent is entering his home board safely and you are throwing high dice. That is the reason five men back is preferable to four, as it enables you to run with the fifth man, yet still keep two points blocked on your opponent's home board. Even though your opponent has a chance a knock off this fifth man, if he is a good player, he will think twice, knowing well enough that if your high dice continue you will eventually have to open one of the two points on his home board. In this case your chances of completing a back game successfully are minimized.

chapter eight

The Rules of Backgammon

The rules of backgammon serve the same function as the rules created for any other game. They exist to avoid rather than to create arguments. The official Rules of the International Backgammon Association appear below.

1. The game is played by two people.
2. Play of the men is governed by two dice, thrown (cast) from a cup in which the dice are shaken before casting.
3a. For the first game, either player may ask to roll for choice of seats, men, dice. Otherwise, they just sit down, set the men up, and play.
3b. At the start of any later game, either player may ask to mix the dice. In this case, he shakes the four dice together in one cup and rolls them out. The opponent selects a die, then the roller, then the opponent, with the roller taking the last one.

THE THROWS

4. For the opening throw, each player throws a single die. Every tie requires another opening throw. Whoever throws the higher number wins, and for his first move plays the numbers upon both dice. After that, each player in turn throws two dice.
5. The dice must be rolled together and come to rest flat (not "cocked") upon the boards at the player's right, otherwise they must be thrown again.
6. There must be a rethrow if a throw is made before an adversary's play is completed or if either player touches a die before it comes to rest.
7. A play is deemed completed when a player moves his men and starts to pick up his dice. If he starts to pick them up before playing all numbers he legally can, his opponent has the right to compel him to complete or not

to complete his play. A roll by the opponent is an acceptance of the play as made. (See rule sixteen.)

THE PLAY

8. The play of the men consists in:

(a) moving a man (or men) the exact number of points indicated by the number on each of the two dice thrown;

(b) entering a man, in the adversary's home board, on a point corresponding to the number on a die thrown;

(c) bearing off a man in the player's home board, when no man is left outside that board or on the bar, in accordance with rule fourteen.

9. Doubles require four plays of the number on the dice.

10. Plays must be made for both dice if possible. Either number may be played first. If either number thrown may be played, but not both, then the higher number thrown must be played.

11. No play may be made which lands on a point held by two or more of the opponent's men.

12. When a play lands on a point occupied by a single man of the opponent's, such a man is hit and must be lifted from the board and placed on the bar for entry in accordance with rule eight.

13. A player having a man on the bar may not play any other man until that man has entered.

14. When in a position to bear off, you may bear off a man from a point corresponding to the number on a die thrown or from the highest occupied point which is lower than the number indicated by a die. If a number is thrown for an unoccupied point, no man below can be borne off, for such number, while any man remains on a higher point. You are not required to bear off a man if you are able to move a man forward on the board. Rule ten applies here as in all other situations.

ERRORS

15. If an error has been made in the setup it must be corrected if either player notices it before the second play of the game has been completed.

16. If an error in play has been made, either player my require its correction before a subsequent throw, but not thereafter.

SCORING

17. A game is won by the player who first bears off all his men.

A gammon (double game) is won if the adversary has not borne off a single man. This doubles the count.

A backgammon (triple game) is won if the adversary has not borne off a single man and has one or more men in the winner's home board or upon the bar. This triples the count.

18. *Doubling game.* The count is raised:

(a) *Automatically*: Each tie of the opening throw doubles the previous count. Unless an understanding has been reached as to the method and limitation of automatic doubles they are not played.

(b) *Voluntarily*: Either player may offer the first optional double of the previous count. After that, the right to double the previous count alternates, being always with the player who has last accepted the double.

In every case, a double may be offered only when it is the player's turn to play and before he has thrown the dice. A double may be accepted or declined. The refusal of a double terminates the game, and the player refusing loses whatever the count may amount to before the double was offered.

The rules of the International Backgammon Association are subscribed to by most of the foremost players in the world. They are in force at the annual tournaments held at Grand Bahama Island and at Las Vegas. Essentially, they derive from the rules prepared in 1931 by the Backgammon and Cards Committee of the Racquet and Tennis Club of New York City.

chapter nine

Doubling

The doubling block, also called a doubling cube, is a square die larger than the dice rolled in the game. It is used to double the stakes for which you play. On each face of the cube are numbers: two, four, eight, sixteen, thirty-two, sixty-four. Doubling blocks are made of different materials such as opaque plastic, ivory, wood, precious metals, or clear plastic. Some are octagonal in shape.

There are now doubling blocks manufactured that start with the number one. And there are backgammon boards made with three holes on the side of the board, or right in the bar, into which the doubling block fits. This eliminates the possibility of the block sliding off the board.

The use of the doubling block was invented in this century to add ano'her gambling element to the game. Middle Eastern players are not familiar with its use.

The proper handling of the doubling block is a very important part of the game both in money and tournament playing.

HOW TO USE THE DOUBLING BLOCK

During the course of the game one player may gain a small strategic and mathematical advantage through a series of favorable dice rolls. The player must then consider doubling.

If he decides to do so, he turns the doubling block, which has been placed in the center of the bar with the number sixty-four facing up, so that the number two is facing up. He then places the cube on the frame that surrounds the board to the left of his opponent. He says, "I double."

The opponent should then think whether the doubler's position is too advantageous to take the risk of accepting the double.

If the double is accepted, the game will be played for double the stakes originally set. In other words, if you were playing for one dollar a game, the stakes are now two dollars a game.

Generally speaking, a double given early in the game can be accepted more readily than later, when a more definite advantage has been established.

One other thing to consider is the fact that should the double be accepted, the person doubling cannot double the next time. The doubling block is now "in control" of the player accepting the double. In other words, if the acceptee now throws a series of advantageous rolls (for instance, a series of doubles), and in turn finds himself ahead and in a more advantageous position to win the game, he may then say to the original doubler, "I double."

The cube would then be turned to number four. Should the player accept the double, the stakes are then four times the original.

One can see that during a game where the advantage shifts back and forth, the game could be played for eight, sixteen, thirty-two, or even sixty-four times the original stakes.

There are several other things to keep in mind when it comes to doubling. If the opponent feels he is too far behind and doesn't wish to accept the double, he then says, "I don't take it." The player giving the double wins the game and the stakes and marks this on the score sheet.

People who enjoy figuring odds and who are mathematically inclined should bear in mind the chances they have of winning the game when they are doubled. If the disadvantage of losing one game is only slight, the double may be taken because even though the odds are against the player at that moment, the fact that the doubling block is in his control reduces these odds.

A player accepting a double should also, before deciding, make fairly certain that he cannot lose a gammon (double game) or a backgammon (triple game).

In considering whether or not to accept a double, keep in mind that the average player has a tendency to accept a double that is not really advantageous. He will chance it, hoping for a roll of good doubles (fives or sixes), which would put him ahead. Of course, a backgammon player wouldn't be a good player if he didn't possess a certain amount of the gambling spirit. However, if' the double is chancy, consider that your opponent's chances for rolling the double sixes or fives are the same as yours. The only thing that might change this fact is if your dice are running hot. If such is the case you could risk the double. But, if the game is up to eight on the doubling block, refuse it.

Often an average player will double after an extremely lucky roll. If your opponent does this, you should never take the double. It often will create a mental block in your mind and prevent you from playing effectively.

Following is a list of factors to keep in mind in deciding whether to accept or refuse a double.

Backgammon

1. Is the opponent a good or bad player?
2. Is he unpredictable?
3. Does he have the habit of refusing close doubles?
4. Are the stakes high enough for him to care?
5. What is the score at that point?
6. Is his position overwhelmingly advantageous?
7. Is the player hot or cold that day?

When the game has reached the point where both players are bearing off, as in the following illustration, the doubling strategy is particularly crucial.

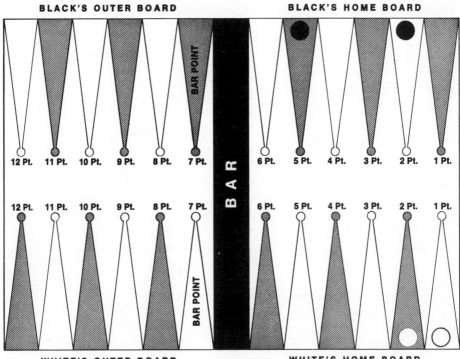

In this situation, Black with one man on his five-point and one man on his two-point (or if his position is better) should double. His chances of throwing the proper combination to bear off are in his favor.

chapter ten

Tournament Backgammon

I. ELIMINATION TOURNAMENTS

There is no question that backgammon tournaments have proven to be an important factor in increasing the popularity of the game. The competitive element in man's nature is attracted by a tournament, and the possibility of winning large sums of money offers an irresistible challenge and stimulates even greater interest.

Backgammon is no different than any other game or sport in that it is very easily adaptable to tournament playing. In fact, it is perhaps more versatile than any other game because it is adaptable to several different types of tournaments.

Elimination tournaments are best run for brackets of 16, 32, 64, 96, 128, 192, or 256 players. It is better to have a few less than these numbers, giving several players "by." These tournaments are run in the same way as tennis and golf elimination tournaments. Opponents are picked out of a hat and after winning their first round, proceed into the second round, and so on until the finals, when one person wins.

In order to make selection of players more impersonal, each player is numbered, and the numbers are pulled from a hat to see who plays whom.

Depending on the time involved after the first round of matches, the points for which each succeeding round is played should be increased.

Since doubling is such an important part of the game, it is highly recommended that all tournaments include the use of the doubling block.

Much experimentation has gone into determining the length of a game of backgammon. In some two hundred games played by players of average speed, it has been found that a game lasts between six and eight minutes. Quite naturally, if there are sixteen players, the first round should be played at for seven points. (First man winning seven or more points wins the round.)

Backgammon

If there are sixty-four players involved, there are two additional rounds to be played. Therefore, the first round should be won at five points.

In large tournaments, which can go on for four or five days, it is a practice to start the first round at thirteen to fifteen points, increasing this by two points each succeeding round. Starting these rounds at fifteen points would of course emphasize the element of skill more significantly.

In a social club tournament where one evening or afternoon is set aside for a tournament of some sixty-four players, it is recommended that the first round should be played for five points, with the semifinals and finals played for seven points. If properly arranged and run, this should take around three or four hours. A time limit should be set for each round and the backgammon committee should rule not to let any round last longer than forty-five minutes. If the two participants are tied at the time, a shake of the dice establishes the winner, with the player rolling the highest dice winning.

The tournament committee, however, can decide whether one more game should or should not be played, depending on whether or not the score indicates that a possible winner could be established after this game.

All players participating should have in mind that backgammon is a fun social game and they should be "good sports." Conversation should be kept to a minimum, as it may upset an opponent. Kibitzer friends should not watch the game and make comments during the round. A player making a wrong move can be helped by kibitzer friends through prearranged signals. Inexperienced players should keep this in mind always. A general list of tournament rules and method of play should be available at the registration desk for all players.

A set of suggested rules and regulations for tournaments follows.

1. All entries are subject to approval by the tournament committee.

2. Players in the beginners' tournament will not be auctioned off.

3. For each player entered, twenty-five dollars will be allotted to the cash prizes and auction pool.

4. Players are requested to move their pieces with only one hand.

5. Players are expected to be punctual in beginning a round and to play at a pace considered "comfortable."

6. A time limit on any round may be imposed.

7. Due to the fact that a backgammon tournament is a pleasant social occasion, players are expected to be cordial and forbearing as well as competitive. For this reason, players are requested to play in comparative silence.

8. Judges may be assigned to any round, and all rounds in the Championship Flight from the quarterfinals up will be assigned judges. Any player may request that a judge supervise a round.

9. At the conclusion of any game, any player may ask that the dice be put in a cup, rolled out together, and an alternate choice of dice be made

before the start of the next game. The player making the request is allowed first choice.

10. If any difference of opinion arises, all men shall be left "status quo" until a judge is rotified. He, with one or more members of the committee, will make any necessary decision. No contesting of play will be considered after the next throw has been made.

11. *Cocked dice:* If a die is not rolled out flat, both dice must be recast. A player may not offer a double before recasting as a play is considered begun when the dice are cast, cocked or not. If a die lands flat on a man, it is considered cocked.

12. *Premature cast:* If a player casts his dice before his opponent has completed his move, the dice must be recast.

13. *Scoring:* Both players should keep score. This rule will not be enforced if both players agree that only one shall keep score.

14. *Spectators:* Any spectator may be barred from watching a round. All spectators are expected to maintain silence during play.

15. In any dispute, the decision of the judge or the judge's committee shall be final.

The tournament committee should be briefed by the chairman as to how to interpret the above rules and should make each ruling in a decisive and yet polite manner.

In "one session" club tournaments, a modest entrance fee should be charged, and after the expenses of the tournament have been deducted, the money should be divided between the winner and the finalist on a 70–30 per cent basis.

If time allows, a second chance for a "consolation flight of players" can also be played. This is composed of all losers in the first and second rounds. The prize money is distributed as above. The consolation flight winner receives 30 per cent while the championship flight winner receives 70 per cent.

The major backgammon tournaments, which last several days, have several consolation flights composed of players defeated in the previous day's play.

Trophies can be given for winners, finalists, and even for players winning semi- or quarterfinal rounds.

Through years of tournament playing, a workable arrangement of seating has evolved. Rows of long tables are set up. On each one, backgammon boards are placed approximately one foot apart. An ashtray should be placed on each side, and a small scorepad and pencil should be on each player's right side. The backgammon committee should see that the tables are kept clean at all times and that personnel is available to do this. The scoreboard is most easily visible by all players if this seating arrangement is employed.

Below is a diagram of the setup of the International Backgammon Association's championship tournaments.

Backgammon

| 8 bg boards | 8 bg boards | 8 bg boards | 8 bg boards |

scoreboard

registration

Tournament Backgammon

A diagram of the tournament scorecard and -board is illustrated below:

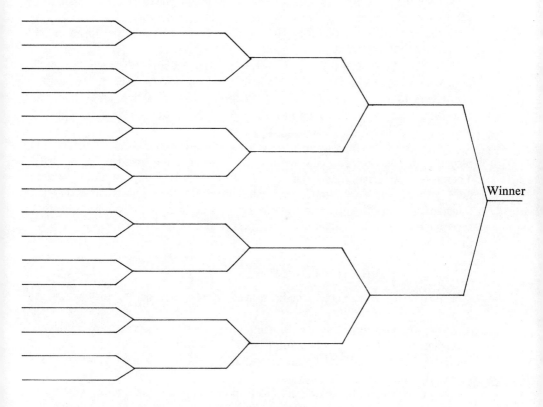

Backgammon

Clubs or groups holding weekly tournaments can add incentive and increase attendance by giving a special prize at the end of each year to the player winning the most rounds for that year. Each player receives one point for each round won. The player winning the largest number of single rounds wins this special prize. A small portion of each tournament's receipts can be deducted for this purpose.

As for the time of day to start one-session tournaments, it is recommended that this be either at two in the afternoon or at nine in the evening. If people are having lunch or dinner at a club, a fifteen-minute, a five-minute, and a one-minute warning should be sounded. Any player not showing up after a ten-minute grace period should be defaulted.

There is no question that luck plays a bigger part in elimination tournament play than in matches between two people simply playing together for money. Therefore, you must adjust your style of play accordingly. Lean more toward luck in determining your moves in such a tournament. Statistics show that in tournaments, average players rolling good dice win more often than the superior players. This encourages the average player and increases his interest in the game.

II. ROUND ROBIN TOURNAMENTS

This type of tournament can be played by any number of players or at home.

Large round robin tournaments: Time allowable for this type of tournament is a factor. If played for the duration of an afternoon or evening, players should be sitting at long tables, one side of which is named "North," the other "South."

Each table should be numbered. North players remain stationary, and South players move to the next highest number after each match. Players sitting at the highest number move all the way to the other end of the table at the lowest number.

Each player plays four matches. These should be composed of three games each. The total number of points won should be placed on the scoreboard opposite the player's name. The one accumulating the most points at the end of the four matches wins the tournament.

In this type of tournament, the doubling block should not be used, for even if the number of doubles is limited, the winning of one triple game could win the tournament.

Round robin tournament play: Experience has proven that in order to win such a tournament, you must win two or three double or triple games. For instance, in the case of playing four matches at three games each, the average winner should have approximately thirteen or fourteen points. This means he must win over four points per match.

Gauge your style of play accordingly, and take more chances than you would in an elimination-type tournament. Also bear in mind that losing a double or triple game is not a catastrophe. This type of tournament takes less skill than any other type.

Another way to run a round robin tournament is to make it last for several days. For instance, if there are fourteen players, have each player play each of the other thirteen during that period for a specified number of points, using the doubling block. Each win is scored as one point, and the player receiving the most points wins the tournament.

III. DUPLICATE TOURNAMENTS

These shouldn't be played with more than fourteen or sixteen players, because they would take too long to finish. In these tournaments, seven or eight tables are set up. Each table is numbered and each side named "North" or "South." One person rolls the dice at the end of the room where the tournament takes place and calls out the numbers rolled in turn for North and South. This continues until the game is completed.

The movement around the table is the same as for a round robin tournament.

A limit of two doubles should be put on each game, and after four matches the players with the most points win the tournament. The reason why this kind of tournament is very entertaining is because of the variety of results at each table. All players make their moves differently. It also makes for improvement of one's game, as the moves can be discussed later.

chapter eleven

Chouette

Another interesting variation of the game of backgammon is called chouette. It is particularly suited to beginners because poorer players have a better chance of winning. A good player can lose a high game, and may have to spend the rest of the session redeeming the loss. Good players do not generally enjoy this type of play, because they cannot use their skill to best advantage and do not have complete control over their game.

Chouette is also a more social form of backgammon. The game is played by more than two players, either three or four. For the purpose of illustration we will use four players. All participants roll but one die. The player rolling the highest number is "in the box." The man rolling the second highest number is called the "captain." He plays the man in the box. The third highest roll plays the first game's winner. The fourth man plays the winner of the second game.

The winner of each game is always the man in the box. If there are any ties in the rolls, the dice are rerolled by the tied men to determine their positions.

The man in the box is now playing against three players as far as scoring goes. If he loses a one-point game, he loses one point to each of the other three men. If he wins, each of the other three loses one point to him.

If the man in the box wins, he plays the next highest die player, who now becomes captain. If he loses, the captain becomes the man in the box. The man formerly in the box becomes the low man.

The captain can ask the advice of his partners in determining his moves. However, he has the final say as to how the move should be made.

The man in the box plays alone and cannot confer with the others.

A double offered by the captain can be accepted or rejected by the man in the box.

A double offered by the man in the box can be accepted or rejected by any one of the partners. If, for instance, the captain refuses to double and his other two partners accept the double, the captain loses to the man in the box whatever count existed before the double. The next man in line then plays as the captain and remains so should he lose that particular game.

Chouette is played usually for no more than four players. If more than four play, the fun of the game diminishes because no one player gets to play frequently enough.

Any additional players coming into the game, at any time, come in at the bottom of the line.

The Official Rules of the International Backgammon Association for the game of chouette follow:

1. Chouette is played by three or more players.

2. In beginning the game, each member shall throw a die. The one throwing the highest number is the "man in the box," the next highest is the "captain." The other members, in accordance with each one's throw, rank below the captain and succeed him in that order.

3. The initial throw shall determine each member's position, but in the event of a tie, only those tying throw again for their position. The highest or higher number always has precedence.

4. Any applicant to chouette may be accepted. He becomes the last-ranking member in the first game in which he participates.

5. After the positions have been determined, the man in the box and the captain proceed as in the two-handed game except that all the remaining members are partners of the captain.

6. The man in the box plays alone and scores separately with each one of his adversaries. He retains his position until defeated. In such event, he retires as a player and takes his place as last-ranking member (unless there be an added member). The captain then becomes the man in the box.

7. The captain may consult with any or all of the partners on any question that may arise in the course of the game. He is, however, the final arbiter, except as hereafter provided. Should he be defeated, he loses his position and takes his place as last-ranking member (unless there be an added member). The highest-ranking partner then becomes captain.

8. All partners are bound by the action of the captain except in the case of a double by the man in the box. In this case any player has the right to refuse or accept the double, irrespective of the action by the captain.

9. Should the captain decline to accept a double offered by the man in the box, he loses his position, and forfeits to the man in the box his count previous to the proposed double.

10. When a double has been declined by the captain, any or all of the other members may accept it. The highest ranking of those accepting becomes captain until the termination of that game.

11. Accepting or declining a double does not change the rank of any

member when the new captain loses; if the new captain wins, he takes the box.

12. Those players who refuse to accept the double are out of that game and may not be consulted from then on.

In the game of chouette, too much discussion and contention slows up the game. The captain should only ask for advice when he is really in doubt as to the play. Partners should give advice only when they think the captain is overlooking a play entirely or when they want to suggest that he double.

chapter twelve

Psychology and Thinking

While you are learning to become an accomplished player, you must constantly remain conscious of the psychology involved in backgammon. Know your opponent! Is he a gambler? Is he a conservative player? Does he consistently play in the same manner? Is he a heavy drinker? Is he apt to press if he's losing? Is he apt to take a risky late double? Is he apt to refuse it? Is he hot or cold that day? Does he gloat when he wins? Is he a bad mover?

As previously stated, although your skill is paramount in importance, the luck of the dice is an ubiquitous factor. There are times when knowing all of the odds and ascertaining the mathematical possibilities of leaving a certain man open cannot help you at all.

How many times have you left a man open to be hit with a one instead of a three? (Respective odds two to one, as compared to three to two, that the man gets hit.) In such a situation, sometimes you have a "feel," and often this feel proves to be correct. Again, you might leave a three open if in your estimation the play would give you a tremendous advantage. However, use this strategy only in crucial situations. Do not use it generally.

If your opponent is a born gambler, you must adjust your game accordingly. Take more chances than you normally would, but don't take as many as he does. Do not double early in the game. It isn't necessary, as a gambler will take your double later in the game even if it is risky. He will hope for a good series of rolls, forgetting that your chances for good rolls are just as good as his. A gambling opponent plays a selfish game, and does not analyze your game as much as he should. Quite often this type of player will show his nature by shaking his dice harder before he rolls. He usually shows his feelings more. He also takes unnecessary chances. Be careful of such a player when he is hot. Then you should become *super*conservative.

Backgammon

When playing a conservative player, be more aware of his game. He may have a tendency to be overconservative and is apt to pile up more than two men on one point. Be cautious in accepting a double from such a player. He will only double when he feels he has a tremendous advantage.

If you judge that your opponent is of approximately the same skill as you, and that the dice are rolling about the same for both of you, use the doubling block in the same way he does. If an opponent plays in the same manner you do, he will be your easiest opponent. The best dice will always win.

A heavy drinker's game collapses sooner or later. Generally speaking, the one thing you should beware of is to become overconfident while playing a drinking opponent. Don't abuse your confidence. Play your usual game and let him make his own mistakes. He will and you will win.

As for your approach to backgammon, confidence is the rule. If you are a good player and show confidence, you will befuddle your opponent. Also, if you are playing against a good player, display as much confidence as you can. Bluff it, if need be. Remember that even though he may be an excellent player he is human and can make mistakes. He is also subject to luck. Don't let him intimidate you. Time and time again, a great player will sit down at the table with great aplomb and try to impress his opponent. He often will, through his relaxed manner and casual approach to the game. You can approach your opponent in the same way.

Further, try to keep an open mind. If you are a beginner or an intermediate player, don't get into a rut. Don't play one certain style. Continually try to improve your game. One way to learn is by playing with and observing the games of people who play better than you do. Notice that often you won't agree with a play they have made. However, keep in mind that they may have made this play for a special reason. Perhaps it is the best move to make in a bad situation. Study these moves. A good player makes them for his own experienced reasons.

If you see a game in process and one player is burning with fury, realize that it is the game and *not* the opponent who has driven him to this state. People have been known to become so upset that dice have gone out the window and entire backgammon boards have been thrown into roaring fireplaces. If this should ever happen to you, don't consider it a personal affront. It is strictly the game.

Apparently there is no way of determining just what kind of person will be a good backgammon player. Oswald Jacoby, for instance, the bridge expert, is also an expert backgammon player. However, other bridge experts have been known to flounder disastrously at backgammon.

It seems that a person who has a good sense of mathematical chance should do well at the backgammon board. However, this too is often dubious. Computers have been known to play very badly when confronted with human experts.

Psychology and Thinking

An outstanding backgammon player should be possessed of a good sense of the luck of the dice, a good, solid knowledge of and experience with the game, and a shrewd appraisal of his own game. Perhaps the most important factor in determining a good player is his knowing exactly when to play and exactly when to quit.

chapter thirteen

Playing for Money

Now the part that you've been waiting for, playing for money. One of the best ways to improve your game is to play for money. Nobody likes to lose money, whether in a game, in the stock market, or on the street, and for this reason you will play your best game when money is involved.

You should always play for the maximum stakes that you can afford to lose. This subconsciously makes you "care" and concentrate very carefully on what you are doing, how you are moving your men, and giving or taking doubles. Money play is quite different from tournament play. When you are involved in a tournament, although the ultimate prize may be cash, cash does not hang on each and every game.

In money play, each point represents a certain sum. If you can afford to play for ten or for one hundred dollars a point, and you are actually playing for twenty-five cents a point, you will not concentrate on your game. You will take unnecessary chances and unnecessary doubles just to see how the game will turn out. This is human nature and the reason also why high-stake players are generally better players than those who play for low stakes. Players who usually play for ten dollars a point and find themselves in a game at twenty-five cents a point will invariably lose the game.

In the following discussion, it is assumed that you will be playing for the highest stakes you can afford to gamble.

If you take chances, such as leaving men open, take them as close to the beginning of the game as is feasible. If you take them later on, minimize the odds of being hit as much as is possible. Do not try to keep a fast pace, as you might well overlook a correct move. At the same time, don't play too slowly, especially if you are losing money. You will have less time to win your money back.

Be more aware than usual as to how you stand in the game. Are you ahead? Are you behind? If so, by how much? What is the score? If you are substantially ahead on the score, you may take a chance you wouldn't ordinarily take.

Although safety first is a good axiom to follow, do not go overboard and pile up five or six men on one point.

Bring builders around and place them in positions that will enable you to make various points with a great variety of throws. In other words, if you already have two builders that will make a point with a three-and-one roll, try not to place your men so that you will have a choice of another three-and-one point if you can possibly bring a man around with the same roll to create a point with a three-and-two roll.

In the long run, a player basing his game on minimizing the odds will win. This, of course, is not the only factor. Strategy and the overall play are important.

Few players possess the same temperament. Some will gloat when they win. Some may be upset when they lose. Human nature doesn't usually allow us to keep these feelings to ourselves. If a player is in a losing streak, he *must* minimize his losses. This is true in any form of gambling. Limit your losses and never limit your winnings. In other words, if you find your dice running cold, don't take chancy doubles. If you are in a winning streak, do just the opposite.

The best thing to do when you are losing is to lay off for a few days. When you are winning, play as much as you can.

A good money player never gets upset. There is always the next game. It is no different than if you have had a bad hole in a golf game. There is always the next hole.

Several years ago, two exceptional players were approaching the end of a game. They were playing for two hundred dollars a point. Player A was, at that stage of the game, thirty-four points behind. He doubled his opponent from an eight to a sixteen game. In order to win the game, player B had to roll a minimum of a five and four. He quietly thought for two minutes, then took the double. The odds of rolling this combination or better were stacked against him. He rolled a six and five and then went on to win the game. He won by fifty points or ten thousand dollars. In deciding to take the double he realized that should he roll the proper combination he would be ahead thirty-two points or sixty-four hundred dollars. He also knew that he was hot that day and that his opponent was cold. He also knew that his opponent would be very upset by being fifty points behind. This would give him an additional edge for the rest of the session. All things considered, he took the double. He came out of the session winning over twenty-five thousand dollars.

As far as backgammon goes, the ageless axiom "Never gamble with strangers" couldn't be more true. If you don't know how a person plays, start with small stakes and later adjust accordingly.

All money matters in backgammon should be settled immediately after a session. If this isn't done, a chain reaction can start among players with only IOU notes exchanged.

Never increase your stakes when losing, and especially if you are already playing for your maximum stakes. The chance of getting into deep water is not worth it. Several high-stake players have done this and lost an entire years' winnings in one session.

Should you be a loser, take it in stride. There's always another game. If you're a good player, your winnings and losings will eventually average out.

Above all, learn to know just how good you are. Never play an expert for a long period of time, thinking that you will clip him. You may beat him in a few games, but you will never come out on top in the long run.

For some of us, it is hard to judge capabilities of other players. Ask friends whose opinions you respect about other players' abilities.

When you are playing for money and there is little difference in the score, the situation may occur that one of the two players in a two-handed game, or one of four or five in chouette, may fall far behind. This situation will affect the mood of the game. The person behind will take risky chances and bad doubles. If you are on the winning side of this coin, consider that you have a good chance of winning even more. If you are losing, keep in mind the basic thought in all forms of gambling. *Minimize your losses.* The average person will almost always think his luck or the odds will change in his favor. Odds do not change. Luck sometimes does. However, psychologically you are almost certainly bound to make mistakes and lose more.

Most backgammon fans play in their own community. And in this community there are always beginners, intermediates, and advanced players. Learn to feel where you fit in and then never play head to head or maximum stakes against someone who is better than you are.

In some circles, clubs, or areas, when playing for money it is sometimes the custom to impose an automatic double if on the first roll both players throw the same dice. A limit should be placed on the number of times these automatic doubles may take place. In addition to this, the game is also played with an automatic double when the first player rejects his first roll. He may take the double and roll again. The opponent can do the same when his turn comes.

As far as automatic doubles are concerned, it is far better to play for higher stakes than to use automatic doubles.

One more comment on playing for money. *Never, never* become a backgammon player who gambles and makes a living out of the game. Somewhere along the line, you will get caught playing over your head and have a tough time paying off. The sleepless nights and long days of anguish as to how you are going to pay off your debts simply are not worth the easy money.

If you are playing backgammon with complete strangers somewhere away from your home base, it is sheer insanity to play for high stakes. Regardless of how you may feel about the people or the place, always play for whatever low stakes are to you. This may mean one dollar a point, or it may mean ten dollars a point. This is a good way to test your opponent's skill. However, be cautious, for he may be playing a bad game purposely, waiting to get into higher stakes. Should this happen to you, casually either drop the stakes or stop playing.

And further, if you do not know your ground, *beware of hustlers!* One of the most audacious examples of hustling occurred a few years ago to one of the top players in the world. In the middle of the game, he excused himself to go to the john and upon returning noted that double fours had been moved while he was gone. Speaking of crust!

Women are prone to hustlers as they are to fortune hunters. This type of hustler will usually escort one or two ladies around and eventually will start teaching them the game. The stakes will be low, twenty-five or fifty cents a point. When these women become fascinated with the game, the stakes go up. They think they are getting good at the game and play. This is the point where the hustlers take over. Before long, these women have lost sizable amounts of money.

The situation may be slightly different for one lonesome female soul. She may have been playing the game for several years, though she hasn't improved very much. Her ego may have been built up, she may need companionship, and twenty-five to fifty dollars a point may not mean much to her. The hustler involved may have great charm and a dazzling personality. He will also egg her on and flatter her game. She may win at first. However, before long, she will get clipped as well.

Hustlers abound in the game of chouette. Silent partners may be splitting the stakes. You may find yourself in a four-handed game with yourself as the sucker. These hustlers may even ask your advice on moves and so forth, splitting the stakes behind your back. In the long run, they'll get you, because it is all planned strategy.

A far better way to play chouette is to declare partners at the beginning of the game. In this way, all is aboveboard and nobody gets hurt.

Another type of hustler may very well be "in" in your social circle. He will use his position in a very civilized manner. However, eventually he will find a sucker. He usually keeps the pigeon to himself, not spreading him around unless he has to. He plays head to head once in a while, and will play in chouette with him. Mr. Sucker is allowed to win a little money here and there and to win a sizable amount every now and then. However, the hustler is keeping a running tab on the amount won and lost. This may go on for months or years. In the long run the sucker may lose a sizable amount of money over a long period of time.

Occasionally, as in all gambling games, hustling takes on a sinister tone. In one case it had a surprise ending. One of the great players was in Europe with a friend. One of the boys from the crime syndicate approached them and suggested a game with two Middle Easterners who were staying at the resort. The game was set, and the two Middle Easterners played the great player's friend. Middle Easterners are not familiar with the use of the doubling block in backgammon. And these two, despite their great confidence in their ability and their backing from the crime syndicate, had little familiarity with the use of it. The friend had skill but little money. With even dice and the friend's skill with the doubling block, he walked off with nine thousand dollars.

Easy prey for not only the hustler, but the advanced player as well, is the "club" champion. Most players who have won a club tournament will have an inflated idea of their game. They are easy marks for the great player, the pro, and the crook. It is advisable to avoid succumbing to the flattery of being challenged by the great players. Wait until you are as solid as the Rock of Gibraltar before taking on this kind of serious competition.

chapter fourteen

Variations of the Game of Backgammon

MOULTEZIM

In this game of Turkish origin, both players come their men in the same manner. The game is distinctly different from conventional backgammon in that men are *not* sent home. The primary strategy should be to create a prime in order to block your opponent. Following this, running and bearing off are in order.

The play starts with each player rolling one die. Highest roll wins the first play. The winner then rolls two dice to determine his first move.

Both players must get to their own outer board with their first man before moving a second man from the starting point.

Two setups for the game are illustrated below.

Backgammon

SETUP NUMBER ONE

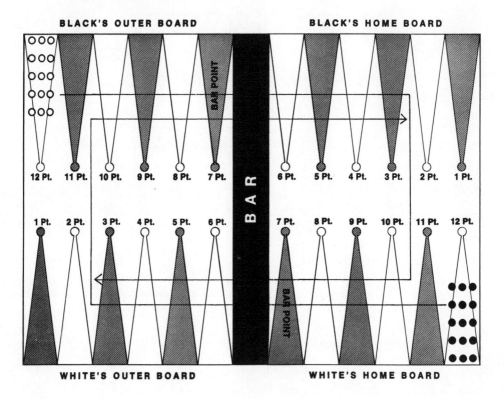

SETUP NUMBER TWO

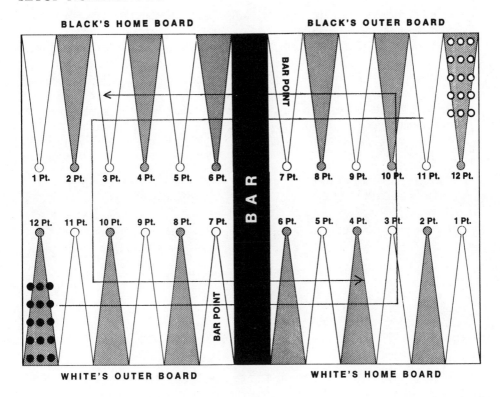

BLACK'S HOME BOARD   BLACK'S OUTER BOARD

BAR POINT

1 Pt. 2 Pt. 3 Pt. 4 Pt. 5 Pt. 6 Pt.   B A R   7 Pt. 8 Pt. 9 Pt. 10 Pt. 11 Pt. 12 Pt.

12 Pt. 11 Pt. 10 Pt. 9 Pt. 8 Pt. 7 Pt.   6 Pt. 5 Pt. 4 Pt. 3 Pt. 2 Pt. 1 Pt.

BAR POINT

WHITE'S OUTER BOARD   WHITE'S HOME BOARD

Backgammon

A sample game of moultezim

White has won the first roll. He rolls six and five. White moves one man from his starting point (Black's twelve-point) to Black's one-point.

Black then rolls four and six. Black moves one man from his starting point (White's twelve-point) to White's two-point.

White then rolls two and six. White moves a two from Black's one-point to his own eleven-point, and a six from his starting point to Black's six-point. Because he has one man on his outer table, White can now start moving all of his men out from his starting point. Black, in turn, must situate his man on White's two-point on his own outer board before he can start moving any of his back men out.

BLACK'S HOME BOARD   BLACK'S OUTER BOARD

WHITE'S OUTER BOARD   WHITE'S HOME BOARD

LOGIC: In moultezim, one man on any spot is a point. Men are *not* sent home. You do *not* stop on top of any man.

The key to strategy in this game is to create a prime in order to block your opponent. However, one of the rules of the game is that you cannot create a prime commencing at the starting point of your opponent. In this section of the board you must leave one point open. In other words, you must have a break in your prime.

Obviously, you should try to get as many men as possible moving from your starting point. In so doing, you will have more men available to play with and consequently will have more of a chance to create a prime along the way.

To create a prime on your opponent's home board is ill-advised, for by the time he brings his men to his outer board waiting to come in, you are farther from home than he is.

PLAKOTO

In Greece, several different variations of the game are played. The game of backgammon as we know it here is called *portas* in Greek, meaning "doors." Each point is a *porta*. A closed door is implied.

The game of plakoto is distinctive in that you can stop on an opponent's man but you cannot remove him from the board. You leave your man on him and he cannot move until you move your man off. Here, as in moultezim, the point is to bear off your men as soon as possible and at the same time prevent your opponent from doing so by landing on his men and immobilizing him.

In the game of plakoto, the board is set up as follows:

SETUP NUMBER ONE

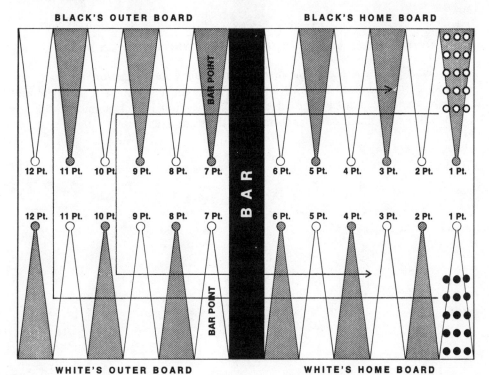

SETUP NUMBER TWO

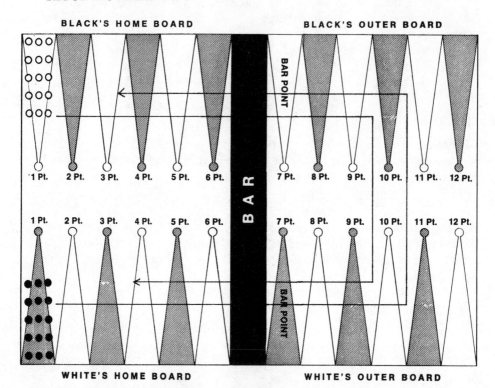

The highest roll makes the first move. In this game, because your man can become immobilized by your opponent's landing on him, it is much more risky to leave a man exposed than in conventional backgammon. Making points is also much more important for the same reason.

Variations of the Game of Backgammon

A sample game of plakoto

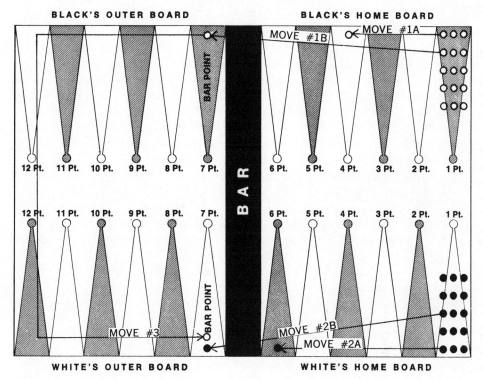

BLACK'S OUTER BOARD **BLACK'S HOME BOARD**

MOVE #1B MOVE #1A

BAR POINT

12 Pt. 11 Pt. 10 Pt. 9 Pt. 8 Pt. 7 Pt. 6 Pt. 5 Pt. 4 Pt. 3 Pt. 2 Pt. 1 Pt.

B A R

12 Pt. 11 Pt. 10 Pt. 9 Pt. 8 Pt. 7 Pt. 6 Pt. 5 Pt. 4 Pt. 3 Pt. 2 Pt. 1 Pt.

BAR POINT

MOVE #3 MOVE #2B MOVE #2A

WHITE'S OUTER BOARD **WHITE'S HOME BOARD**

White opens with a six and three, moving one man from Black's one-point to Black's four-point, and one man from Black's one-point to Black's bar point.

Black rolls a six and five, moving one man from White's one-point to White's six-point, and one man from White's one-point to White's bar point.

White then rolls a six and five. He moves his man on Black's bar point to his own bar point, covering Black's man on White's bar point.

LOGIC: Black's man is now immobilized for practically the duration of the game, certainly at least until White has all of his men home. White should move this cover man as late as possible in the game. He should win a double game.

167

GIOUL

The game of gioul originated in Turkey. The board is set up as in the game of plakoto and the men are moved in the same direction.

One man stopping anywhere is considered a point, while six men in a row constitute a prime. Men are not sent home as in backgammon.

The basic difference between this game and others mentioned in this section lies in the rolling of doubles. When a player rolls doubles, he plays them as in backgammon, but then continues playing the next number of doubles all the way to double sixes. For example, if double ones are thrown, the player first plays the double ones, followed by double twos, double threes, double fours, double fives, and double sixes.

If double threes are thrown, the player plays the double threes, followed by double fours, double fives, and double sixes.

All of these moves are made before the opponent makes his next roll. Playing consecutive doubles at the beginning of the game presents no problems. However, as the game progresses and the opponent has made points (simply by placing one man on any spot), it often occurs that the player cannot complete all of his doubles. In that case he forfeits the rest of his doubles to his opponent.

For example, assume that one man has rolled double threes. He is able to play the double threes and double fours, but cannot play double fives, or can only play one double five. The opponent will then complete playing the fives and also play the double sixes. If, in turn, the opponent is unable to finish the double sixes, the play is completed and the opponent makes a new roll.

Gioul takes longer to play than other variations of backgammon, because moves are made constantly with the idea of preparing for a double throw. Planning and strategy are based on this chance. Blocking opponent's double sixes becomes very important. Placing men in a position to be able to move double sixes becomes important as well.

EUREIKA

Eureika is a very simple game, taught to children at an early age in the Middle East to accustom them to setting up a backgammon board. After they have mastered this game, they are taught the variations described above.

The game is a game of 100 per cent luck. There is no skill involved.

Each player places two men each on his four-point, five-point, and six-point, and three men each on his one-point, two-point, and three-point. One die is thrown by each player, with the highest number playing first.

As each roll is made, a man is slid off in front of the corresponding number on the home board. The object of the game is to get all men off.

Glossary

BACK GAME—A type of game played when one finds himself so far behind that he must concentrate on getting more men back (usually four or five) and must forget his running game.

BACKGAMMON—When a player has borne off all of his men and the opponent still has at least one or more men stranded in the winner's home board or on the rail, the victor scores three times the value of the game, or a backgammon.

BAR—The space which separates the home board and the outer board, running from one player's side to the other's. Sometimes this is a raised partition.

BAR POINT—The first point in the player's outer board, next to the bar, labeled the seven-point in the diagrams.

BEARING OFF—The final stage of the game, when a player has moved all his men to his home board and begins to remove them according to the rolls of the dice.

BLOCK—Any point on the board where two or more men rest. An opponent may not land on such a point.

BLOCKING GAME—A defensive game, played when your opponent's dice have been better than yours, and when he is playing a running game.

BLOT—A space with only one man on it. A vulnerable situation, for if the opponent makes a throw that lands one or more of his men on the space, the man is sent off the board. The man must then re-enter and begin again.

BOARD—The term is used in two ways. First, the entire backgammon table is called the board. Secondly, the four divisions within the tables are called outer boards and home boards.

Glossary

BOX—A term used in chouette. The man who has rolled the highest number is said to sit "in the box." The other players play against him.

BREAKING A PRIME—The process of removing a man or men from a point in a side prime or prime.

BUILDER—A man brought down close to your home board as an extra man. With him, you may hope to make an additional point in your home board or just outside your home board.

CAPTAIN—A term used in chouette. The player rolling the second highest number and the man who plays the man in the box.

CHECKERS—One word used for the discs moved on the board. Not preferred.

CHOUETTE—A type of backgammon in which more than two people play. One man competes against the others, who constitute a team. One member of the team, representing the others and calling on them for advice, plays against the single man.

COME IN—Bringing a man back into play, after having been hit, or knocked off.

COME ON—A term used synonymously with "come in."

COUNTERS—The discs used to play the game. This is the preferred term.

CUBE—The cube marked with the numbers 2, 4, 8, 16, 32, and 64 used to double the stakes.

CUP—The cup used to throw the dice. It should have a small lip on the inside to prevent fixing the dice.

DOUBLE—Increasing the stakes of the game to twice their immediately previous size.

DOUBLES—A roll of the dice in which both dice show the same number. A player plays each die twice.

DOUBLING BLOCK—The block used to signify the double.

DOUBLING CUBE—A word used synonymously with doubling block.

EXPOSED MAN—A man who sits alone on a point. He is vulnerable to being hit if the opponent lands on the same point.

GAMMON—When a player has borne off all his men and the opponent still has not borne off any, the victor scores twice the value of the game, or a gammon.

HALF A ROLL—The measure of the distance one man is ahead of another. Thus, if you have no men borne off and your opponent has three off, if it is your shake, your opponent is a roll and a half ahead of you. If it is his shake, he is two and a half rolls ahead of you.

HIT—Landing on a blot, and subsequently sending the man off the board.

HOME BOARD—A player's own one- through six-points.

HOME TABLE—The same as above; however, not the preferred term today.

INNER BOARD—The same; however, not the preferred term today.

INNER TABLE—The same; however, not the preferred term today.

KNOCK OFF—The same as hit.

LOVER'S LEAP—The opening 6/5 move in which a player moves one man eleven points.

MEN—Used synonymously with counters.

OFF THE BOARD—Where a man is sent when he is hit, or knocked off.

OUTER BOARD—A player's bar through twelve-points.

OUTER TABLE—The same as above; however, not the preferred term today.

POINTS—A term used in two ways. First, each of the long, triangular shapes on the board are called points. There are twelve of these on each side of the board. Second, any of the above-defined points on which two or more men of one color rest. If two or more men are on one point, a player may move more of his own men to that point. However, the opponent may not move onto any point so occupied.

PRIME—Six successive or adjacent points anywhere on the board, occupied by points of one player.

RAIL—A word used synonymously with "off the board."

RUNNING GAME—The offensive backgammon game, a tactic utilized by the man who has thrown the best dice.

SAFE—Landing a second man on a blot, thus making a point.

STAYING BACK—A defensive strategy leading to playing a back game.

TABLE—A word used synonymously with board. Not preferred today.